A. B. SIMPSON
His Life and Work

Formerly "The Life of A. B. Simpson"

BY

A. E. THOMPSON, M.A.

CHRISTIAN PUBLICATIONS, INC.
3825 Hartzdale Drive
Camp Hill, PA 17011

Portrait of A. B. Simpson at the age of Sixty-five.

A. B. Simpson

His Life and Work

ISBN 0-87509-044-3

FOREWORD

THE author of this book undertook a very difficult work in writing the life's story of Dr. A. B. Simpson, one of the great spiritual leaders of the last century. To be merely factual would fall short of the readers' expectations. Any attempt to rationalize would rob it of its spiritual impact and deny the supernatural in the life and work of this Christ-centered personality. We cannot overlook the influence of a good home, hard work, self-discipline, and divine providences. If this were done, some might be tempted to suspect the author of trying to glamorize and canonize our founder. But he has done neither. He has instead endeavored to show the hand of God in and upon a single life whose words and works have enriched the whole church in the whole world.

Dr. Simpson had a good beginning in life, being born into a Christian home where his life was directed by devout and godly parents. I would particularly commend the chapter, "Personal Reminiscences," to all parents and children. He was richly endowed with many natural qualities and gifts which were destined to make him a notable leader in the religious world.

However, the secret of his creative life was related to the spiritual crises into which he came. Aware of the fact that while he preached and taught the deeper things of the Word of God, his own heart had not experienced them until the day he took from the shelf and read from an old musty volume on the subject of the fuller Christian life. It was not a conclusion at which he arrived, but a revelation to his consciousness. His theology then became a fire in his heart.

With this unveiling came the burden for the spiritual life of the church of God and the evangelization of the lost. Many came to realize the fulness of their privileges in Christ and identified themselves with Dr. Simpson. His message was timely and transforming. Organizations were formed which ultimately became known as The Christian and Missionary Alliance. This was not a protest movement, but a fellowship with a distinctive message.

Spiritual personalities all over the world pay tribute to the influence of the spoken message and the written word of this man of God. His ministry turned tens of thousands toward the life that is Christ's, world service that is sacrificial, and the hope that will sustain and strengthen until the day dawn and the shadows flee away.

He was a cultured Christian gentleman, a poet, a great pulpiteer, a wise counsellor, and a sympathetic friend. His forceful missionary sermons kindled a fire in the hearts of his hearers and changed viewpoints about world-wide evangelization. He was endowed with the unusual ability of taking Old and New Testament Scriptures and making one see Christ and His life as his personal privilege and possession.

Today, though dead, he speaks through his writings. Today transformed lives of men and women and the witness of pastors and missionaries all over the world are a testimony to the creativeness of Dr. Simpson's anointed ministry. We would to God that his mantle might fall upon another and this generation might hear the voice of a great spiritual leader that would change the course of church history.

DR. R. R. BROWN, *Pastor*
OMAHA GOSPEL TABERNACLE
OMAHA, NEBRASKA

ON EAGLE'S WINGS.

Mounting up with wings as eagles,
  Waiting on the Lord we rise;
Strength receiving, life renewing,
  How our spirit heavenward flies!
Then our springing feet returning
  To the pathway of the saint,
We shall run and not be weary,
  We shall walk and never faint.

Oh, we need these heights of rapture
  Where we mount on eagle's wings;
Then returning to life's duties,
  All our heart exultant springs.
This our every burden lightens
  Till, with sweet, divine constraint,
We can run and not be weary,
  We can walk and never faint.

—A. B. Simpson.

CONTENTS

CONTENTS

CHAPTER 1

A HOUSEHOLD OF FAITH

ALBERT B. SIMPSON came of generations of sturdy and upright stock and was reared in surroundings congenial to the development of noble and godly character. The "Bonnie Highlands" of Scotland is the home of a race as rugged as its rocky hills, yet as sensitive as its matchless lakes to the moods of wind and weather. Neither Roman legions nor Saxon knights ever subdued those haughty, crafty clansmen, and on every battlefield of modern nations the tartan and bonnet of "The Kilties," marching to the weird skirl of the pibroch, have been in the hottest of the fray. As widely scattered, as easily recognized, and as successful as the sons of Jacob, some one has sung of them,

> "They thrive where'er they fall.
> Oh, grasp the hardy thistle close,
> Or grasp it not at all."

Nor need young Canada, his own much loved native land, be abashed even in the presence of the Highlands. As Dr. Simpson himself said in a lecture, delivered both in his native island and in the church where fifty years before he had been ordained, "Every Canadian seems by his very attitude to be forever saying, 'I can.' His life story will reveal many influences, all instrumental in the making of a life of rare completeness. But it would be a very faulty interpretation that overlooked the effects of his ancestry and early environment. For the seeds of character are the fruit of a family tree, and the home

and the community are as soil and sunlight to the young
life.

The Simpson family emigrated from Morayshire, Scotland, and settled in Prince Edward Island in 1774. James
Simpson, the grandfather of Albert B. Simpson, was then
a boy of five years. In after years he married a daughter
of the island and reared a family of seven boys and four
girls. The fourth boy, James, married Jane, the daughter
of William Clark, who with his wife was also of Scottish
ancestry, being descended from the Covenanters. He
was a member of the legislature, and on his death, his
son William, then only twenty-one years of age, was
elected to his seat, which he carried in every election till
he was eighty years old. The family is still widely known
and greatly respected.

Jane Clark's maternal grandmother, Mrs. McEwan, a
very godly woman, told her tales of the persecutions her
people had suffered at the hands of Claverhouse and his
dragoons; of their faithfulness to the truth amid the
fiercest persecution; of Peden, the prophet, and other
great preachers; of the secret conventicles among the
hills where these godly folk worshiped at the risk of
their lives; of miracles of deliverance, and of the final
triumph of the Reformers in Scotland. No more thrilling chapter has been written in Church History, and
the heart of this high-minded girl was stirred to a passion of devotion to the faith of her fathers and the
God whom they worshiped.

Nor was James Simpson less earnest in his consecration to Christ than the young lady whom he sought as his
helpmeet. Carefully instructed in the great truths for
which his forefathers had bled, and converted at the age
of nineteen, he became an earnest student of the Bible.

Though away from home during the years of his early manhood and cast among godless companions who scoffed at his religion, he continued true to his convictions and steadfast in his Christian life. He stood at the marriage altar a clean, capable, industrious, and prosperous young man, worthy of the remarkable woman whose heart he had won.

The iron crane was hung in the home of James and Jane Simpson in Bayview, Prince Edward Island, on February 1, 1837. Here five of their nine children were given to them. Albert Benjamin, the fourth child, was born on December 15, 1843. The firstborn, James Albert, was taken away when only two and a half years old. William Howard and Louisa were older than Albert, and Margaret Jane two years younger. It was a happy home, and sunny skies smiled upon it.

James Simpson had established himself as a shipbuilder, miller, merchant and exporter. He carried on his business in connection with the Cunard Steamship Company, exporting the product of his mills—flour, oatmeal, and pearl barley—and importing British goods which he sold in his store to the farmers for their produce. Such a medium of exchange was a necessity, and the business prospered till the financial depression which tested the foundations of British commerce swept over the empire. Shipbuilding was suspended, and export trade was threatened with extinction. James Simpson sold his business and with part of the proceeds bought a farm in western Ontario.

Miss Louisa Simpson, the last surviving member of the household, gives us the following intimate sketch of the journey to their new home and of the family.

"When my father moved to this country in 1847, he

chartered a sailing vessel, and taking with him seven families, some of whom had worked with him in his large business, crossed the Gulf of St. Lawrence and sailed up the river. At Montreal he took a boat for the Great Lakes. From Detroit a river boat brought us up the Thames to Chatham. It was a journey of thrilling pleasure to me. Albert, then three and one-half years old, was sick all the time, and it was a great trial to him. On his arrival at Chatham, father at once bought valuable property and settled us in a nice home, intending to remain permanently and enter into partnership with a shipbuilder in town; but our little sister took ill and died in an epidemic which nearly depleted the town of its infants; and my mother, in dread for the rest of the children, insisted on going to the farm nine miles away, not caring what the hardships might be if only she could save her three remaining children from death.

"Father was not a farmer, and it was a hard struggle for him, but he was very courageous and with hired help he soon cleared the farm. Being an excellent carpenter, he converted the log house into a comfortable home and with his own hands made beautiful furniture from the walnut on the farm. My mother decorated the home and surrounded it with beautiful flowers. A few years later a new house and fine farm buildings were erected. The surrounding country was gradually transformed into the garden of western Ontario.

"While speaking of my father, I feel that I owe it to his memory to say that in a period ranging from my babyhood till he was nearly eighty-five years of age, I never once saw him lose his temper or say an unkind word to anyone, though I often saw him hurt deeply, for he was very tender and most affectionate. His life was ra-

diant with sunshine. As my brother James, who lived
on the farm, stood with me beside father's coffin, he said
almost enviously, 'There lies a man who never wronged
his fellow.'

"Mother was a most earnest Christian all her life. She
was a woman of the highest ideals. I could add a long
list to the names of her favorite poets which my brother
has mentioned. In fact we had about all the poets worth
while in our little library. What Albert says in his sketch
regarding her sensitive nature and poetic temperament
is emphatically true. Deeply religious, she trained us
to take everything to God in prayer. When I was not
more than six years old, I used to talk to Jesus and tell
Him everything as if He were really present in person.

"With such parents ours was a very happy home. The
children who were brought to the farm and the others
who were born there made a large family circle. Albert
was very timid and imaginative, and anything unusual
left a deep impress upon his memory. The thought of
punishment would fill him with terror. I never saw him
get a whipping; and if he ever got one, it was very tenderly administered. He had been devoted to the Lord
in his infancy, but my parents withheld this knowledge
from him as they felt that God alone had any right to
influence him in this matter.

"Howard was four years older than Albert. He was
shy, sensitive, affectionate, a great lover of flowers and
of everything beautiful, a brilliant student and a writer
of many poems of considerable merit, yet he thought
nothing of his own attainments. His thirst for knowledge
was insatiable, and he would stand beside his father at
his work all day and ply him with questions. He was
always delicate, probably as the result of being burned

almost to death when less than three years old, and he contracted an illness during his last pastorate in Frankfort, Indiana, necessitating his retirement from active work while still in middle life and his return to Chatham where he died August 22, 1888.

"James Darnley was born on the farm, and there he spent his life. Sturdy and healthy, he was generous to a fault. Albert when writing to my father spoke of him as 'my noble brother James.' He united mother's high ideals and father's beautiful disposition. His conversion was very similar to Albert's, his conviction of sin being terrible, and his peace, when at last it came, was most profound. He lived wholly for others, helping them in their bodily needs in order to reach their souls.

"Peter Gordon, our youngest brother, was a carpenter and builder. In temperament he was mathematical rather than literary. He was delicate in health and died at the age of forty-seven.

"We had a little sister, Elizabeth Eleanor, born on Albert's birthday, December 15, 1852, of whom he was exceedingly fond, but she was taken from us when less than four years old. A baby brother died at birth.

"And now the family tree has but one leaf left, and that is fluttering in the breeze ready to drop—the little sister and helper of the rest—and soon all will meet above an unbroken family, not one missing."

CHAPTER 2

PERSONAL REMINISCENCES

A T the urgent request of friends, Dr. Simpson began an autobiography and wrote a few pages, sketching in his racy style some of the events of his early years. His disinclination to speak of himself, which was a noteworthy characteristic, overcame him, and he left us only what follows in this chapter and a few paragraphs which appear in the story of his college days.

"The earliest recollection of my childhood is the picture of my mother as I often heard her in the dark and lonely nights weeping in her room; and I still remember how I used to rise and kneel beside my little bed, even before I knew God for myself, and pray for Him to comfort her. The cause of her grief I afterwards better understood. In that lonely cabin, separated from the social traditions to which she had been accustomed and from all the friends she held so dear, it was little wonder that she should often spend her nights in weeping, and that her little boy should find his first religious experiences in trying to grope his way to the heart of Him who alone could help her.

"I would not leave the impression that my beloved mother was not a sincere and earnest Christian, but she had not yet learned of that deep peace, which came to my own heart later in life, and which alone can make us independent of our surroundings and conditions. She was of a sensitive and highly poetic temperament. Her favorite reading was old English poets. She delighted in Milton, Pollock, Thompson, Kirke, White, and others of that highly imaginative school, and I am sure that I have inherited a certain amount of inspiration from her lofty nature.

"My next reminiscence has also a tinge of religion about it. I had lost a boy's chief treasure—a jack-knife, and I still remember the impulse that came to me to kneel down and pray about it. Soon afterwards I was delighted to find it. The incident made a profound impression upon my young heart and gave me a life-long conviction, which has since borne fruit innumerable times, that it is our privilege to take everything to God in prayer. I do not mean to convey the idea that I was at this time already converted. I only knew God in a broken, far-away sense, but I can see now that God was then discounting my future, and treating me in advance as if I were already His child, because He knew that I would come to Him later and accept Him as my personal Saviour and Father. This perhaps explains why God does so many things in answer to prayer for persons who do not yet know Him fully. He is treating them on the principle of faith, and calling 'the things that are not as though they were.'

"The truth is, the influences around my childhood were not as favorable to early conversion as they are today in many Christian homes. My father was a good Presbyterian elder of the old school, and believed in the Shorter Catechism, the doctrine of foreordination, and all the conventional principles of a well ordered Puritan household. He was himself a devout Christian and most regular in all his religious habits. He was an influential officer in the church and much respected for his knowledge of the Scriptures, his consistent life, his sound judgment, and his strong, practical common sense. I can still see him rising long before daylight, sitting down with his lighted candle in the family room, tarrying long at his morning devotions, and the picture filled my childish soul with a kind of sacred awe. We were brought up according to the strictest Puritan formulas. When we did not go to church on Sunday in the family wagon, a distance of nine miles, we were all assembled in the sitting room, and for hours father, mother, or one of the older children read in turn from some good old book that was far beyond my understanding. It gives me a chill to this day to see the cover of one of those old books, such as Boston's *Fourfold State,* Baxter's *Saints' Rest,* or Doddridge's *Rise and Progress of Religion in the Soul,* for it was with these, and such as these, that my youthful soul was disciplined. The only seasons of relief came when it happened to be my turn to read. Then my heart would swell with pleasure, and I fear with self-conscious pride, and for a time I would forget the weariness of the volume. In the afternoon we all had to stand in a row and answer questions from the Shorter Catechism. There were about one hundred and fifty questions in all. Our rule was to take several each Sunday till they were finished, and then start over again and keep it up from year to year as the younger children grew up and joined the circle.

"My good father believed in the efficacy of the rod, and I understood this so well that I succeeded in escaping most dispensations of that kind. One of the few whippings, however, which I remember, came because one Sabbath afternoon, when the sun was shining and the weather was delightful, I ventured to slip out of the house, and was unfortunately seen by my father scampering 'round the yard in the joy of my ungodly liberty. I was speedily called back and told with great solemnity that I would get my whipping the next morning after breakfast, for it was not considered quite the thing to break the Sabbath even by a whipping. I got the whipping that was coming to me all right the next morning. But I still remember how my elder brother, who had a much wider experience and a deeper mind than I, took me aside that day and told me that if I was ever condemned to a whipping, he knew a way of getting out of it. Then he told me with great secrecy that if such an occasion should arise, to get up that morning before daylight, a little before my father was accustomed to rise, light the candle, and go and sit in a corner of the sitting-room with the big Bible before me, showing a proper spirit of penitence and seriousness. He had found by experience that my father would take the hint and let him off. I am sorry to say that my heart was as yet sufficiently unsanctified to take the hint, and sure enough one morning when a whipping was coming to me, I stole out of my bed and sat down with a very demure and solemn face to practice my pretended devotions. I can still see my quiet and silent father sitting at the table and casting side glances at me from under his spectacles as though to make quite sure that I was truly in earnest. After finishing his devotions, he quietly slipped away to his work, and nothing more was said about the chastisement.

"Looking back on these early influences, I cannot say I wholly regret the somewhat stern mould in which my early life was shaped. It taught me a spirit of reverence and wholesome discipline for which I have often had cause to thank God, the absence of which is perhaps the greatest loss of the rising generation today. It threw over my youthful spirit a natural horror of evil things which often safeguarded me afterwards when thrown as a young man amid the temptations of the world. The religious knowledge, which was crammed into my mind even without my understanding it, furnished me with forms of doctrine and statements of truth which afterwards became illuminated by the Holy Spirit and realized in my own experience, and thus became ultimately the precious vessels for holding the treasures of divine knowledge. In our later family history these severe restraints were withdrawn from the younger members as a new age threw its more relaxing influence over our home; but I cannot say that the change proved a beneficial one. I believe that the true principle of family training is a blending of thorough discipline with true Christian liberty and love.

"My childhood and youth were strangely sheltered and guarded by divine providence. I recall with sacred awe many times when my life was almost miraculously preserved. On one occasion, while climbing up on the scaffolding of a building in course of erection, I stepped upon a loose board which tipped over and plunged me into space. Instinctively throwing out my hands, I caught a piece of timber, one of the flooring joists, and desperately held on, crying for assistance. When exhausted and about to fall, a workman caught me just in time. The fall would certainly have killed me or maimed me for life.

"At another time I was thrown headlong over my horse's head as he stumbled and fell under me. When I came back to consciousness, I found him bending over me with his nose touching my face, almost as if he wanted to speak to me and encourage me. At another time I was kicked into unconsciousness by a dangerous horse, and still remember the awful struggle to recover my breath as I thought myself dying.

"Once I had a remarkable escape from drowning. I had gone with one of my schoolmates in the high school to gather wild grapes on the banks of the river. After a while my companion tempted me to go in swimming, an art about which I knew nothing. In a few moments I got beyond my depth, and with an agony I shall always remember, I found myself choking under the surface. In that moment the whole of my life came before me as if in a vision, and I can well understand the stories told by drowning persons of the photograph that seems to come to their minds in the last moment of consciousness. I remember seeing as clearly as if I had read it from the printed page, the notice in the local newspaper telling of my drowning and the grief and sorrow of my friends. Somehow God mercifully saved me. My companion was too frightened to help me, but his shouts attracted some men in a little boat a short distance away, and they pulled me out just as I was sinking for the last time, and laid me on the river bank. As I came back to consciousness a while afterwards, it seemed to me that years had passed since I was last on earth. I am sure that experience greatly deepened my spiritual earnestness.

"But, like other boys, I often passed from the sublime to the ridiculous as this little incident will show. It was my good fortune to secure as a first prize in the high school an extremely handsome book which my chum, who had failed in the examination, had set his heart upon getting. He finally succeeded in tempting me by an old violin, which he used to practice on my responsive heart, until at last I was persuaded to exchange my splendid prize for his old fiddle. The following summer I took it home and made night hideous and myself a general nuisance. I had never really succeeded in playing anything worth while, but there must have been somewhere in my nature a latent vein of music, and still to me the strains of the violin have a subtle inspirational power with which nothing else in music can be compared.

"My first definite religious crisis came at about the age of fourteen. Prior to this I had for a good while been planning to study for the ministry. I am afraid that this came to me in the first instance rather as a conviction of duty than a spontaneous Christian impulse. There grew up in my young heart a great conflict about my future life; naturally I rebelled against the ministry because of the restraints which it would put upon many pleasures. One irresistible desire was to have a gun and to shoot and hunt; and I reasoned that if I were a minister, it would never do for me to indulge in such pastimes.

"I was cured of this in a somewhat tragic way. I had saved up a little money, earned through special jobs and carefully laid aside, and one day I stole off to the town and invested it in a shot gun. For a few days I had the time of my life. I used to steal out to the woods with my forbidden idol and then with my sister's help smuggle it back to the garret. One day, however, my mother found it, and there was a never-to-be-forgotten scene. Her own brother had lost his life through the accidental discharge of a gun, and I knew and should have remembered that such things were proscribed in our family. It was a day of judgment for me; and when that wicked weapon was brought from its hiding place, I stood crushed and confounded as I was sentenced to the deep humiliation of returning it to the man from whom I bought it, losing not only my gun but my money too.

"That tragedy settled the question of the ministry. I soon after decided to give up all side issues and prepare myself if I could only find a way to preach the Gospel. But as yet the matter had not even been mooted in the family. One day, however, my father in his quiet, grave way, with my mother sitting by, called my elder brother and myself into his presence and began to explain that the former had long been destined to the ministry and that the time had now come when he should begin his studies and prepare to go to college. I should say that at this time we both had an excellent common school education. My father added that he had a little money, rescued from the wrecked business of many years before, now slowly coming in, which would be sufficient to give an education to one but not both of his boys. He quietly concluded that it would be my duty to stay at home on the farm while my brother went to college. I can still feel the lump that rose in my throat as I stammered out my acquiescence. Then I ventured with broken words and stammering tongue to plead that they would consent to my getting an education if I could work it out without asking anything from them but their approval and blessing. I had a little scheme of my own to teach school and earn the money for my education. But even this I did not dare to divulge, for I was but a lad of less than fourteen. I remember the quiet trembling tones with which my father received my request and said, 'God bless you, my boy.'

"So the struggle began, and I shall never cease to thank God that it was a hard one. Some one has said, 'Many people succeed because success is thrust upon them,' but the most successful lives are those that began without a penny. Nothing under God has ever been a greater blessing to me than the hard places that began with me more than half a century ago, and have not yet ended.

"For the first few months my brother and I took lessons in Latin, Greek and higher mathematics from a retired minister and then from our kind pastor, who was a good scholar and ready to help us in our purpose. Later I pursued my studies in Chatham High School, but the strain was too great, and I went back to my father's house a physical wreck. Then came a fearful crash in which it seemed to me the very heavens were falling. After retiring one night suddenly a star appeared to blaze before my eyes; and as I gazed, my nerves gave way. I sprang from my bed trembling and almost fainting with a sense of impending death, and then fell into a congestive chill of great violence that lasted all night and almost took my life. A physician told me that I must not look at a book for a whole year for my nervous system had collapsed, and I was in the greatest danger. There followed a period of mental and physical agony which no language can describe. I was possessed with the idea that at a certain hour I was to die; and every day as that hour drew near, I became prostrated with dreadful nervousness, watching in agonized suspense till the hour passed, and wondering that I was still alive.

"One day the situation became so acute that nothing could gainsay it. Terrified and sinking, I called my father to my bedside and besought him to pray for me, for I felt I was dying. Worst of all I had no personal hope in Christ. My whole religious training had left me without any conception of the sweet and simple Gospel of Jesus Christ. The God I knew was a being of great severity, and my theology provided in some mysterious way for a wonderful change called the new birth or regeneration, which only God could give to the soul. How I longed and waited for that change to come, but it had not yet arrived. Oh, how my father prayed for me that day, and how I cried in utter despair for God to spare me just long enough to be saved! After that dreadful sense of sinking at last a little rest came, and the crisis was over for another day. I looked at the clock, and the hour had passed. I believed that God was going to spare me just one day more, and that I must strive and pray for salvation that whole day as a doomed man. How I prayed and besought others to pray, and almost feared to go to sleep that night lest I should lose a moment from my search for God and eternal life; but the day passed, and I was not saved. It now seems strange that there was no voice there to tell me the simple way of believing in the promise and accepting the salvation fully provided and freely offered. How often since then it has been my delight to tell poor sinners that

> "We do not need at Mercy's gate
>   To knock and weep, and watch and wait;
> For Mercy's gifts are offered free,
>   And she has waited long for thee.

"After that, as day after day passed, I rallied a little, and my life seemed to hang upon a thread, for I had the hope that God would spare me long enough to find salvation if I only continued to seek it with all my heart. At length one day, in the library of my old minister and teacher, I stumbled upon an old musty volume called *Marshall's Gospel Mystery of Sanctification*. As I turned the leaves, my eyes fell upon a sentence which opened for me the gates of life eternal. It is this in substance: 'The first good work you will ever perform is to believe on the Lord Jesus Christ. Until you do this, all your works, prayers, tears, and good resolutions are vain. To believe on the Lord Jesus is just to believe that He saves you according to His Word, that He receives and saves you here and now, for He has said—'Him that cometh to me I will in no wise cast out.' The moment you do this, you will pass into eternal life, you will be justified from all your sins, and receive a new heart and all the gracious operations of the Holy Spirit.'

"To my poor bewildered soul this was like the light from heaven that fell upon Saul of Tarsus on his way to Damascus. I immediately fell upon my knees, and looking up to the Lord, I said, 'Lord Jesus, Thou hast said—Him that cometh to me I will in no wise cast out. Thou knowest how long and earnestly I have tried to come, but I did not know how. Now I come the best I can, and I dare to believe that Thou dost receive me and save me, and that I am now Thy child, forgiven and saved simply because I have taken Thee at Thy word. Abba Father, Thou art mine, and I am Thine.'

"It is needless to say that I had a fight of faith with the great Adversary before I was able to get out all these words and dared to make this confession of my faith; but I had no sooner made it and set my seal to it than there came to my heart that divine assurance that always comes to the believing soul, for 'He that believeth hath the witness in himself.' I had been seeking the witness without believing, but from the moment that I dared to believe the Word, I had the assurance that

> 'The Spirit answers to the blood
> And tells me I am born of God.'

"After my health was restored, I secured a certificate

as a common school teacher, and at the early age of sixteen I began teaching a public school of forty pupils.
One-quarter of the pupils were grown up men and women
while I looked even younger than my years and would
have given anything for a few whiskers or something that
would have made me look older. I often wonder how
I was able to hold in control these rough country fellows,
but I can see that it was the hand of the Lord, and He
was pleased to give me a power that did not consist in
brawn or muscle. My object in teaching was to earn
money for my first cycle of college, and along with my
teaching I was studying hard every spare moment between times to prepare for the first examination of my
college course.

"The months that followed my conversion were full of
spiritual blessing. The promises of God burst upon my
soul with a new and marvelous light, and words that had
been empty before became divine revelations, and every
one seemed specially meant for me. I think I had inherited from my mother a vein of imagination, and it
clothed the glowing promises of Isaiah and Jeremiah with
a glory that no language could express. With unspeakable ecstasy I read and marked, 'I have sworn that I will
never be wroth with thee, nor rebuke thee; for the mountains shall depart and the hills be removed, saith the
Lord that hath mercy on thee.' When I heard other
Christians talking of their failures and fears, I wondered
if a time would ever come when I should lose this supreme joy of a soul in its earliest love; and I remember
how I used to pray that rather than let me go back to
the old life, the Lord would take me at once to heaven.

"One of the memorable incidents of my early Christian life, of which I still have the old and almost faded

manuscript, was my covenant with God. While I was teaching school, I had been reading Doddridge's *Rise and Progress of Religion in the Soul,* in which he recommends young Christians to enter into a written covenant with God. I determined to follow this suggestion and set apart a whole day to fasting and prayer to this purpose. I wrote out at great length a detailed transaction in which I gave myself entirely to God and took Him for every promised blessing, and especially to use my life for His service and glory. There was a certain special blessing, partly temporal and partly spiritual, which I included in my specifications. I have since often been amazed how literally God had fulfilled this to me in His wonderful and gracious providences throughout my life. and I can truly say after more than two generations that not one word hath failed of all in which He caused me to hope. Before the close of the day I signed and sealed this covenant just as formally as I would have done a human contract and have kept it until this day.

"A SOLEMN COVENANT *

"The Dedication of Myself to God."

"O Thou everlasting and almighty God, Ruler of the universe, Thou who madest this world and me, Thy creature upon it, Thou who art in every place beholding the evil and the good, Thou seest me at this time and knowest all my thoughts. I know and feel that my inmost thoughts are all familiar to Thee, and Thou knowest what motives have induced me to come to Thee at this time. I appeal to Thee, O Thou Searcher of hearts, so

---

*Evidently Dr. Simpson did not intend to publish this covenant, but it is so illuminating that we insert it.

far as I know my own heart, it is not a worldly motive that has brought me before Thee now. But my 'heart is deceitful above all things and desperately wicked,' and I would not pretend to trust to it; but Thou knowest that I have a desire to dedicate myself to Thee for time and eternity. I would come before Thee as a sinner, lost and ruined by the fall, and by my actual transgressions, yea, as the vilest of all Thy creatures. When I look back on my past life, I am filled with shame and confusion. I am rude and ignorant, and in Thy sight a beast. Thou, O Lord, didst make Adam holy and happy, and gavest him ability to maintain his state. The penalty of his disobedience was death, but he disobeyed Thy holy law and incurred that penalty, and I, as a descendant from him, have inherited this depravity and this penalty. I acknowledge the justness of Thy sentence, O Lord, and would bow in submission before Thee.

"How canst Thou, O Lord, condescend to look on me, a vile creature? For it is infinite condescension to notice me. But truly, Thy loving kindness is infinite and from everlasting. Thou, O Lord, didst send Thy Son in our image, with a body such as mine and a reasonable soul. In Him were united all the perfections of the Godhead with the humility of our sinful nature. He is the Mediator of the New Covenant, and through Him we all have access unto Thee by the same Spirit. Through Jesus, the only Mediator, I would come to Thee, O Lord, and trusting in His merits and mediation, I would boldly approach Thy throne of grace. I feel my own insignificance, O Lord, but do Thou strengthen me by Thy Spirit. I would now approach Thee in order to covenant with Thee for life everlasting. Thou in Thy Word hast told us that it is Thy Will that all who believe in Thy Son

might have everlasting life and Thou wilt raise him up
at the last day.   Thou hast given us a New Covenant
and hast sealed that covenant in Thy blood, O Jesus, on
the cross.

"I now declare before Thee and before my conscience,
and bear witness, O ye heavens, and all the inhabitants
thereof, and thou earth, which my God has made, that
I accept the conditions of this covenant and close with
its terms.   These are that I believe on Jesus and accept
of salvation through Him, my Prophet, Priest, and King,
as made unto me of God wisdom and righteousness and
sanctification and redemption and complete salvation.
Thou, O Lord, hast made me willing to come to Thee.
Thou hast subdued my rebellious heart by Thy love.   So
now take it and use it for Thy glory.   Whatever rebellious thoughts may arise therein, do Thou overcome them
and bring into subjection everything that opposeth itself
to Thy authority.   I yield myself unto Thee as one alive
from the dead, for time and eternity.   Take me and use
me entirely for Thy glory.

"Ratify now in Heaven, O my Father, this Covenant.
Remember it, O Lord, when Thou bringest me to the
Jordan.   Remember it, O Lord, in that day when Thou
comest with all the angels and saints to judge the world,
and may I be at Thy right hand then and in heaven with
Thee forever.   Write down in heaven that I have become
Thine, Thine only, and Thine forever.   Remember me,
O Lord, in the hour of temptation, and let me never
depart from this covenant.   I feel, O Lord, my own weakness and do not make this in my own strength, else I
must fail.   But in Thy strength, O Captain of my salvation, I shall be strong and more than conqueror through
Him who loved me.

"I have now, O Lord, as Thou hast said in Thy Word, covenanted with Thee, not for worldly honors or fame but for everlasting life, and I know that Thou art true and shalt never break Thy holy Word. Give to me now all the blessings of the New Covenant and especially the Holy Spirit in great abundance, which is the earnest of my inheritance until the redemption of the purchased possession. May a double portion of Thy Spirit rest upon me, and then I shall go and proclaim to transgressors Thy ways and Thy laws to the people. Sanctify me wholly and make me fit for heaven. Give me all spiritual blessing in heavenly places in Christ Jesus.

"I am now a soldier of the cross and a follower of the Lamb, and my motto from henceforth is 'I have one King, even Jesus.' Support and strengthen me, O my Captain, and be mine forever.

"Place me in what circumstances Thou mayest desire; but if it be Thy holy will, I desire that Thou 'give me neither poverty nor riches; feed me with food convenient, lest I be poor and steal, or lest I be rich and say, Who is the Lord?' But Thy will be done. Now give me Thy Spirit and Thy protection in my heart at all times, and then I shall drink of the rivers of salvation, lie down by still waters, and be infinitely happy in the favor of my God.

"Saturday, January 19, 1861."

Written across this covenant are the following renewals; one of which was made during his third year in college and the other during his second pastorate.

"September 1, 1863. Backslidden. Restored. Yet too cold, Lord. I still wish to continue this. Pardon the past and strengthen me for the future, for Jesus' sake. Amen."

"Louisville, Ky., April 18, 1878.   Renew this covenant and dedication amid much temptation and believe that my Father accepts me anew and gives me more than I have dared to ask or think, for Jesus' sake.   He has kept His part.   My one desire now is power, light, love, souls, Christ's indwelling, and my church's salvation."

CHAPTER 3

THE HIGH CALLING

IT was no easy path that led from the farm on the Ontario lowlands to the pulpit and the manse. In the Presbyterian Church of Canada the ministry was a sacred and carefully safeguarded calling. The church session, the presbytery, the faculty and the senate of the college must all be satisfied as to the fitness of the candidate. Beyond these lay the supreme test, for in the Presbyterian democracy every congregation is a final court of decision as to its minister. He cannot be settled as a pastor until he has "a call" from a congregation, and in those days a call was never extended until a number of candidates had been heard in the pulpit, their merits determined, and a decision reached by vote of the church.

To a devout family no higher honor could come than to have a son in the pulpit, and many were the parents who, like the Simpsons, dedicated their firstborn as an offering to God and the Church. To have another son choose this path was a double honor. Dr. Simpson has given us a vivid picture of the family council when his father announced that Howard, the firstborn, had been dedicated to the ministry, and when he himself informed the family of his own desire. To one member of the circle that confession was no surprise. His sister says: "Like little Samuel, he was given to the Lord from his birth. My mother told me that she gave him to the Lord to use him in life or death; to be a minister and a foreign missionary, if the Lord so willed, and he lived to grow up and was so inclined." He had, in fact, given early indications of his inclination. The children were sometimes left at home when the parents journeyed nine miles to church in Chatham. On such occasions, Albert, when not more than ten years old, would fit up the kitchen table as a pulpit and preach to the rest of the children.

Yet honor meant accountability, and the parents felt a keen sense of responsibility for their full share in the making of a minister. Had their boy the "pairts," as the Scotch termed natural ability? Was the call of God upon him? Had he surrendered earthly joys and ambitions for this heavenly calling? Could the family provide for his education? All this and much more is evident in Mr. Simpson's description of the scene in the family circle where, with fear and trembling, he made known his desires. But when once the decision was made, the family never thought of turning back. The two boys had been the mainstay on the farm, but henceforth they were primarily students and not farmers. The parents made great sacrifices, and the other members of the family joined heartily in the plans for the education of their brothers.

Miss Louisa Simpson, who was older than Albert, recalls the struggle through which they went. "My brothers wanted to study the classics, so my father engaged as tutor a retired minister of the Presbyterian Church, a good scholar, and the boys commenced their classical education and made rapid progress. Later, after their tutor had left, our pastor, the Rev. William Walker, offered to give them lessons twice a week if they could go into town. My father gave them a horse each, and they rode the nine miles to the manse to get their lessons, and thus continued their studies for a length of time.

Shortly afterward Albert thought it would be better to enter the high school at Chatham and give his entire time to study. Howard was in poor health and thought he would have to discontinue his studies, so he engaged as school teacher and taught instead.

"While Albert was in high school, the drowning incident which he has narrated occurred. Shortly afterward, Rev. H. Grattan Guinness, of London, England, visited Chatham, and under his pungent preaching Albert was deeply convicted. Still under conviction he walked home for the week end and was lost in the woods. He wandered upon some Indian graves which had been desecrated, and the gruesome sight greatly affected his sensitive spirit, not yet recovered from the effect of the drowning experience. His father found him and brought him home, but a long illness followed, during which he suffered intense spiritual darkness and often could sleep only with his father's arms about him. It was during this time that he was converted.

"As soon as he recovered, he received his certificate and secured a school and taught till the end of September when he went to Toronto, to Knox College, Howard remaining behind and teaching school another year. Two other members of the family were teachers, and the farm was quite productive, and what was earned or raised was gladly drawn upon to help the boys in their education."

There is an apostolic succession in Presbyterianism which lies deeper than a formal consecration by the laying on of hands—a succession of life, of spirit, of high traditions, of intangible realities. When a lad appears in that succession, it is the crowning glory of a pastor's ministry. Rev. William Walker had the unusual joy of introducing two sons of one of his elders into that fellow-

ship. With the devotion that characterized the godly
minister of the old school, he counseled them, tutored
them, commended them to the presbytery and continued
his friendly offices during their course of preparation for
the ministry.

The presbytery is a court composed of the ministers
within a defined area and a representative elder from
each church session. It is their prerogative to decide
upon the merits of a candidate for the ministry, to accept
him as a catechist, to grant him the privilege of preaching
in the pulpit as occasion offers, to recommend him to the
church college which he wishes to attend, to license him
as a preacher of the Gospel when his course is completed,
and, when he is called to be the minister of a congregation,
to ordain him to the ministry. The old time presbytery
took nothing for granted, nor did it trust the results of
secular educational examinations, nor for that matter
those given by the church colleges. Democratic to an
extreme, it jealously guarded its own honors and insisted
that the candidate, from the day of his first appearance
before it until by its hand he was ordained, should prove
himself and his spiritual and intellectual attainments in
at least an annual appearance before them. By such
means have Presbyterians maintained the high standard
of their traditions.

Albert B. Simpson appeared with other candidates
before the presbytery of London, Ontario, on October
1, 1861. According to custom, they sat in silence while
the presbytery proceeded with its routine business. Presently a committee was appointed for the examination—
and what an examination! Their antecedents, their character, their spiritual experience, their attainments, their
soundness in the faith, and their "call" must all be in-

quired into. When the report was presented to the presbytery, happy were they on finding themselves excused from reading sermons of their own production in this fearsome presence. The presbytery records show that they all passed a creditable examination and were recommended for admission to Knox College, Toronto.

We are curious to learn how a boy of seventeen, almost fresh from a country farm, met the test of filling the pulpits of those old-time Presbyterian churches. Presbyterians are the greatest "sermon tasters" in the world. The pulpit is the glory of the church. They will bear much from their minister if only he fail not when he stands before them to declare the oracles of God.

Albert Simpson's testing was the severest that could have been put upon a boy. During his first Christmas holidays he was asked to preach in Tilbury, near his home. His father, his gifted, emotional mother, who cannot lift her eyes to her boy's face, his brothers, his sister, his playmates, his neighbors are in the audience. There may be a trace of jealousy in the pews, but intense interest is lacking in none. Yesterday he was Bert Simpson, their fellow, their rival in friendly contests of brain and brawn. Today he stands high above them in the pulpit, a minister—no, not yet a minister—but in the minister's place, back of the open Bible where not even his godly father would appear, to speak to them as a messenger of God. Can any one who has formed a part of such a scene ever forget it? The boy, whose voice was to thrill five continents, did not fail. Tense nervousness in pulpit and pew soon changed to tenser interest in the message, for even then the messenger became

"A voice of one crying—
Prepare ye the way of the Lord,
Make his paths straight."

If any vivid imagination pictures his friends crowding around him, they little know an old-time Presbyterian congregation. They had subtler ways of manifesting either approval or disapproval. Albert Simpson expected no effusiveness, and one of the marks of his greatness was that, till the end, he maintained the spirit of his fathers in this regard, never allowing any one to congratulate him on his preaching. In the memorial service in the Gospel Tabernacle, New York, Rev. Edward H. Emett told that a short time before he had linked his arm into Dr. Simpson's, and had begun to tell him how much his preaching had inspired his own ministry. He was quietly but quickly interrupted with the word, "That is all very well, Emett, but tell me something about what Christ has done for you."

His success in the home church was repeated in others, though his boyish appearance sometimes caused embarrassing situations. On one occasion he was following the beadle, who was carrying the Bible into the pulpit, when one of the elders stopped him, and he had difficulty in persuading that worthy official that he was the duly appointed supply for the day.

One of his college friends, Rev. James Hastie, gives us the following account of their first meeting.

"One summer I taught a rural school a few miles from Sarnia, Ontario. The Presbyterian Church was vacant and was hearing candidates. On a certain Sabbath there was no supply, but unexpectedly a handsome lad entered the church and conducted the service. He gave his name as A. B. Simpson. A double surprise came to that Scotch congregation, surprise to see a lad of seventeen years in the pulpit, and still greater surprise to hear that youth preach sermons which in content would do credit to a professor of homiletics, and for diction and delivery would meet the demands of a teacher of elocution. During dinner, a lady from a church some distance away insisted that he repeat in the afternoon a sermon which she had heard him deliver three months before. Mr. Simpson replied that he had not used it since, nor had he the manuscript with him, nor any notes, and therefore he could not recall that sermon with any satisfaction. When she still insisted, the young preacher asked his hostess for the use of a room. In less than half an hour he came out, entered the pulpit, and without a word of explanation to the congregation delivered the sermon asked for, which was fully the equal of the one given in the forenoon in exposition, illustration, searching application, and beauty of diction."

CHAPTER 4

COLLEGE DAYS

K NOX COLLEGE is now situated on the campus of the University of Toronto occupying one of the finest seminary buildings on the continent. It was opened in 1844 in one room when the disruption of the Church of Scotland resulted in a similar division in the Canadian Church. In Mr. Simpson's day, Elmsley Villa, formerly the residence of Lord Elgin, Governor of Canada, located where Grosvenor Street Presbyterian Church now stands, was its home.

In October, 1861, Albert B. Simpson entered Knox College as a student for the ministry. He was brought up in the United Presbyterian Church and had looked forward to attending the denominational seminary in Toronto, but in that year it was absorbed into Knox College when the Canadian Presbyterian Church was formed by the union of the United Presbyterian with the Free Church. He had studied so diligently under his ministerial tutors in high school, and during the time he was teaching that, though he was only seventeen years old, he was admitted to the third or senior year of the literary course. The college required either the full arts course in the University of Toronto, with which it was the first seminary to affiliate, or three years of academic work in its own halls as a prerequisite to the three years' course in theology.

The college staff, though not a large body, was excellent. The head of the Literary Department was Pro-

fessor George Paxton Young, who afterward occupied
the Chair of Philosophy in Toronto University, a man
who is remembered for his brilliant scholarship, his ex-
ceptional ability as a teacher, and his never-failing devotion to his students. The principal of the Theological
Department was Professor Michael Willis. Dr. Robert
Burns, one of the great figures in the church of that day,
was Professor of Church History and Christian Evi-
dences, while Professor William Caven, who was to leave
his mark on Knox College by nearly half a century of
service, was lecturing in his quietly brilliant way in the
Department of Biblical Literature and Exegesis. These
men and their associates were real educators, untouched
by the blight of rationalistic criticism which has fallen
upon many theological professors of our day.

Among the students were J. Munroe Gibson, LL.D.,
who became the most outstanding figure in the Presby-
terian pulpit of London, England; Francis M. Patton,
D.D., a former President of Princeton University;
James W. Mitchell, D.D., Henry Gracey, D.D., James
Hastie, John Becket, George Grant, M.A., and Robert
Knowles, all of whom survived Mr. Simpson; R. N.
Grant, D.D., known in literary circles as Knoxonian;
Mungo Fraser, D.D., one of Mr. Simpson's successors
in Knox Church, Hamilton; and Robert Warden, D.D.,
for many years treasurer of the Presbyterian Church
in Canada.

Dr. J. W. Mitchell, who has followed Mr. Simpson's
career sympathetically, has this to say of his college days:
"My earliest recollections of Dr. Simpson go back to the
early sixties when he came up to Knox. Your photo-
gravure gives a fair representation of him as he then
appeared, fresh from his father's farm and his country

school teaching, giving little intimation of the mighty man of God that he was to become in later years. He did not take a full course at the University. He had popular gifts of a high order, and I opine was eager to get into the field where he could exercise them, and was sure he would forge his way to the front. I was his senior, being graduated in 1863. In that summer, after Simpson's first year in theology, he was assigned to do some work as a student supply. I had recently been licensed and contemplated postgraduate work in Edinburgh after the summer's work in the field. During part of the time we alternated. The field was Welland, Crowland, and Port Colborne. I did my work faithfully and acceptably, but was quite thrown into the shade by my junior, for already his pulpit gifts were notable."

Another of his classmates, Rev. James Hastie, thus describes him: "He was a most attractive young man— his body lithe, active, graceful; his countenance beaming with kindness, friendship, generosity; his voice rich, musical, well controlled. Often, no doubt, flattery was showered upon him, and strong compliments were paid by admirers and relatives, all of which would tend to develop vanity and self-importance; but I never saw a trace of these traits, which are so common in brilliant young men, in young Mr. Simpson. 'Meek and lowly in heart' after the pattern of his divine Master was his characteristic then and subsequently."

Rev. J. Becket, who was also in college with him, writes that "he was a favorite with the students and in urgent request as a preacher of the Gospel." A friend who knew him intimately says that he was never a slavish student, and displayed in his college days the same ability to grasp a theme quickly and, if necessary, to restate it in an

almost offhand fashion which characterized him in his
later years.

Though he entered the third or final year in the academic course, he proved his ability and scholarship during
that first year in college by winning the George Buchanan
Scholarship of $120.00 in a special competitive examina-
tion in the classics. His aptitude in doctrinal discussion
appeared when the next year he received the John Knox
Bursary prize for an essay on "Infant Baptism." One
of his life long characteristics was a love for history.
It is said that he and his brother had read Gibbon's *Rise
and Fall of the Roman Empire* while mere children.
Little wonder, therefore, that he won the Prince of Wales
prize for an essay on "The Preparation of the World
for the Appearing of the Saviour and the Setting Up of
His Kingdom." This prize, open to first and second year
students in theology, was tenable for two years.

The scholarships and prizes which he won were of great
financial assistance. The modest remuneration given for
student supply in the summer added to the little store.
He had to fall back on tutoring in the winter. Even then
he was sometimes in sore straits. Facing an audience in
Grosvenor Street Church in Toronto in 1896, where many
students were gathered, he related one of these experiences. "Many a time I found myself without a penny.
I have thrown myself down on the college lawn, not far
from where I stand, in the darkness of the night and
deeper darkness of soul, crying to God for money to pay
my board bill. And, fellow students, He did not fail
me then, nor has He failed me yet. Neither will He fail
you if you will dare to trust Him." Yet even in such
circumstances, that almost reckless generosity which was
always evident in him would manifest itself. Not long

since his daughter recalled that her father had once confided to her that on one occasion when he had received the then munificent sum of ten dollars as a fee for his Sunday services, he at once proceeded to spend it for a present for his sweetheart.

A few years ago, when called upon to address the students of Toronto University, he captivated his audience by one or two reminiscences of his college days. Then, turning to the young ladies, he remarked that their presence made him feel quite at home, for fifty years before he had left his heart at the door of a Toronto residence as it was opened by the fair daughter of the house.

That was an eventful day. Dr. Jennings, whose church the Simpson brothers attended, had become interested in them, and one day he said to his leading elder, Mr. John Henry, "You have a room that you are not using, and there are two students in Knox who need it. Will you not ask them to call upon you and see what you think of them?" It was this invitation that brought Albert Simpson to the door of Mr. Henry's home and face to face with his eldest daughter, Margaret. Quite unconscious that the boy already had been sorely wounded by Cupid's arrow, the father and mother graciously invited him and his brother to accept their hospitality, with the inevitable result that before the winter was over the fate of two lives was sealed. Margaret Henry as a girl had all the quiet dignity and resourcefulness that she has shown through a long and eventful life as the wife and for fifty years the partaker of the joys and sorrows of one of the great leaders of our time.

Dr. Simpson has left us the following personal reminiscences of his life in college.

"It would be of little interest to recite the ordinary experience of a college student, and it is only necessary to sketch a few of the special pictures that come back to memory from these early years. My deep religious impressions still continued, and they kept me from the temptations of city life. But I was thrown with a roommate in the first year of my college course whose influence over my heart was most disastrous. He was a much older man, and although a theological student and a very bright and attractive fellow, was a man of convivial tastes and habits. It was his favorite custom once or twice a week to have what he called an oyster supper in our room, and to invite one or two of his friends, who happened to be medical students, and whose habits were worse than his. On these occasions both beer and whiskey would be brought in, and the orgy would go on until very late at night with laughter and song and story and many a jest that was neither pure nor reverent. I had not firmness nor experience sufficient to suppress these entertainments, and I was compelled to be a witness, in some measure a partaker, although the coarse amusement was always distasteful to all my feelings. But gradually these influences had a benumbing effect upon my spiritual life. My roommate was cynical and utterly unspiritual. At the same time he had a fine literary taste and was fond of poetry which he was always reading or repeating. There was a certain attraction about him, but altogether his influence over me was bad.

"I did not cease to pray or to walk in some measure with God, but the sweetness and preciousness of my early piety withered. I am sorry to say that I did not fully recover my lost blessing until I had been a minister of the Gospel for more than ten years.* My religious life was chiefly that of duty, with little joy or fellowship. In a word, my heart was unsanctified, and I had not yet learned the secret of the indwelling Christ and the baptism of the Holy Ghost.

"At the same time there must have been a strong current of faith and a real habit of prayer in my college life, for God did many things for me which were directly supernatural and to me at the time very wonderful. There was a system of college scholarships, or bursaries, consisting of considerable amounts of money, which were given to the successful student in competitive examinations. I set my heart on winning some of these scholarships, not merely for the honor, but for the pecuniary value, which would be about sufficient to meet what was lacking in my living expenses. One of them required the writing of an essay on the subject of baptism, and after much hard study, and I am glad to say, very much prayer, I wrote an essay proving to my own satisfaction that children ought to be baptized and that baptism should be by sprinkling and not by immersion. Through God's great goodness I won the prize, but in later years I had to take back all the arguments and doctrinal opinions which I so stoutly maintained in my youthful wisdom.

"My next venture was for a much larger prize, amounting to $120.00, for which an essay was to be written on the difficult historical and philosophical subject: 'The Preparation of the World for the First Coming of Christ and the Setting Up of His Kingdom.' While I studied hard and long for the materials of this paper, I deferred the final composition till the very last moment. I am

*See renewal of Covenant, page 22.

afraid that my mind has always had a habit of working in this way, namely, of leaving its supreme efforts until the cumulative force of constant thought has crystallized the subject into the most intense form. So I found myself within two days of the moment for giving in the papers and the entire article yet to be written out in its final form from the crude first copy which had been prepared.

"The task proved to be a longer and harder one than I dreamed; and when the last day had ended, and the paper had to be given in by nine o'clock the following morning, there was still seven or eight hours' work to be done. Of course the night that followed was sleepless. Toiling at my desk, and literally tearing along like a race horse for the goal, I wrote until my hand grew almost paralyzed, and I had to get another to write for me while I dictated. But soon my brain began to fail me, and I found myself literally falling asleep in my chair. Then for the first and last time in my life I sent out to a drug store for something that would keep me awake for six or seven hours at any cost, and my brain was held to its tremendous task, till as the light broke on the winter morning that followed, the last sentences were finished, the paper folded and sealed and sent by a special messenger to my professor while I threw myself on my bed and slept as if I should never wake.

"Some weeks passed during which I prayed much for the success of my strenuously prepared paper. I found there were about a dozen competitors, some of whom were students in a higher year. There seemed little hope of my success, but something told me that God was going to see me through. At length the morning came when the name of the successful candidate was to be announced. I was so excited that I slipped away to a quiet place in the college yard where I threw myself on my knees and had the matter out with God. Before I rose, I dared to believe that God had heard my prayer and had given me the prize which was so essential to the continuance of my study. Then I returned to the class room and sat down in my place. I instantly noticed that every eye was turned on me with a strange expression which I could not understand. At the close of the lecture my professor called me to his room and congratulated me on my success, and I learned for the first time that while I was out praying in the yard, he had told the class that the prize had come to me. I mention this instance especially to show how all through my life God has taught me, or at least has been trying to make me understand, that before any great blessing could come to me I must first believe for it in blind and naked faith. I am quite sure that the blessing of believing for that prize was more to me than its great pecuniary value.

"During the summer vacations, as I was a theological student, I was sent out to preach in mission churches and stations. In this way I also earned a little money, besides gaining a much more valuable experience in practical work. But I remember well the look of surprise with which the grave men of the congregations where I preached would gaze at me as I entered the pulpit. I was extremely young and looked so much younger than I really was, that I do not wonder now that they looked aghast at the lad who was presuming to preach to them from the high pulpit where he stood in fear and trembling.

"The greatest trial of all these days was my preaching for the first time in the church in which I had been brought up and in the presence of my father and mother.

In some way the Lord helped me to get through, but I never once dared to meet their eyes. In those days preaching was an awful business, for we knew nothing of trusting the Lord for utterance. The manuscript was written in full, and the preacher committed it to memory and recited it verbatim. On this occasion I walked the woods for days beforehand, repeating to the trees and squirrels the periods and paragraphs which I had so carefully composed."

CHAPTER 5

THE FIRST PASTORATE

"WHEN I was a young minister of twenty-one, and just leaving my theological seminary, I had the choice of two fields of labor; one an extremely easy one, in a delightful town, with a refined, affectionate, and prosperous church, just large enough to be an ideal field for one who wished to spend a few years in quiet preparation for future usefulness; the other, a large, absorbing city church, with many hundreds of members and overwhelming and heavy burdens, which were sure to demand the utmost possible care, labor and responsibility. All my friends, teachers and counsellors advised me to take the easier place. But an impulse, which I now believe to have been, at least indirectly, from God, even though there must have been some human ambition in it, led me to feel that if I took the easier place, I should probably rise to meet it and no more; and if I took the harder, I should not rest short of all its requirements. I found it even so. My early ministry was developed, and the habit of venturing on difficult undertakings was largely established, by the grace of God, through the necessities of this difficult position." Such are Mr. Simpson's own reflections on his entry into pastoral work.

Mr. Simpson graduated from Knox College in April, 1865. In June the synod authorized the Presbytery of Toronto to take him and several other candidates on public probationary trial for license.

It may surprise young preachers of our day to know

that the minutes show that this old-time presbytery subjected these college graduates to a searching examination in Biblical Hebrew and Greek, Theology, Church
History, and Church Government, as well as personal
religion. Moreover Mr. Simpson's examination included
a discourse on II Timothy 1:10, read before the presbytery, and the following· papers submitted for criticism:
a Latin thesis, *an filius dei ab eterno sit genitis a Pater;*
an excursus on Romans 7; a popular sermon on Romans 1:16, and a lecture on Matthew 4:1-11. After
this procedure the candidates were licensed as ministers
of the Presbyterian Church of Canada.

But the end was not yet. Mr. Simpson had been urged
by the church in Dundas, which he had supplied after
graduation, to become its pastor. This he declined. On
August 15 a call was presented to him through the presbytery to Knox Church, Hamilton. Upon his acceptance
of it, he was ordered to appear in two weeks with an ar-
ray of sermons and papers similar to those which he had
presented for license, but he was excused from the
scholastic examination which had been given by the Presbytery of Toronto. September 12, 1865, was set as the
day for his ordination and induction.

That was a momentous week in the life of A. B.
Simpson. On Sunday, September 11, he preached his
first sermon as the accepted pastor of Knox Church.
On Monday, at two p. m., ·the presbytery met in Knox
Church for his ordination. Rev. R. N. Grant, a class-
mate, preached; Dr. Ormiston addressed the minister;
Mr. Stark addressed the congregation; and the modera-
tor, Dr. Inglis, offered the ordination prayer as he was
set apart to the ministry by the laying on of the hands
of the presbytery. On Tuesday he was married in To-

ronto to Margaret Henry, daughter of John Henry, by
their pastor, Dr. Jennings, and Rev. William Gregg, of
Cooke's Church, afterwards Professor of church history
in Knox College. The honeymoon was spent in a trip
down the St. Lawrence, and a few days later a hearty
welcome to the manse was given the young pastor and
his bride.

Knox Church had been organized after the disruption
in 1844 when the Free Church element left St. Andrews,
which remained in the "Auld Kirk." A handsome stone
edifice, with a seating capacity of 1200, was erected in
1846. Its first pastor, Mr. Gale, accepted a professorship
in Knox College, as did also one of his successors, Rev.
G. Paxton Young. Mr. Simpson's immediate predeces-
sor was Rev. Robert Irving, D.D., a brilliant preacher.
There were men of great ability in the neighboring pulpits, including Dr. Ormiston, who was called a little later
to New York City; Dr. David Inglis, afterward professor in Knox College and later a pastor in Brooklyn, New
York, and Dr. John Potts, who became the greatest
leader in the Methodist Church of Canada.

To maintain the traditions of such a pulpit was no
easy matter for a young man of twenty-one, yet the
Hamilton Spectator only voiced the judgment of all who
knew this young pastor when, in reviewing the history of
Knox Church, it stated that "He was second to none
in point of eloquence and ability and success in his ministry." Dr. William T. McMullen, who graduated from
Knox College before Mr. Simpson entered, saw him in
the larger relation in the Canadian church. "I was intimately acquainted with Rev. A. B. Simpson, D.D., during his pastorate in Knox Church, Hamilton, which I

judge must be about fifty years ago. He stood out at that time as one of the most brilliant young ministers of our church in Canada. He was endowed with intellect of a very high order, and he preached the Gospel of the great salvation with a gracefulness of manner, a fervor, and a power exceedingly impressive." His great compatriot, Dr. R. P. Mackay, Secretary of the Board of Foreign Missions of the Presbyterian Church of Canada, gives him a higher tribute. "I can recall, when I began my ministry, a young man in Hamilton who was spoken of as 'the eloquent young preacher.' He went to New York, and afterwards I only knew him by reports. Any man who has been able to accomplish so much must have been endowed with special gifts. The quality of his work is the best testimony as to the depth of his spiritual life. Such men do not belong to any one section, but are the gift of God to the Church of Christ."

In those days few Presbyterian ministers engaged in special evangelistic campaigns, however earnest they might be as preachers of the Gospel. Dr. Wardrobe, of Guelph, Ontario, was one of the exceptions. An incident which he recalled in his later years is illuminating. "I had just returned to Ontario from a pastorate in the Maritime Provinces, and, being in Hamilton for a day, I decided to call upon a young preacher there and ask him, as the most likely man I could think of, to come and assist me in a series of revival meetings. With much dignity he replied, 'I believe in the regular work of the ministry.' What was my surprise, therefore, to learn not many years later that my young friend Simpson had left the 'regular work of the ministry' to give himself to the evangelization of the neglected masses of the American metropolis."

No greater evidence of success could be given than the place the minister won in the lives of individuals and in the memory of the congregation. In the memorial service in the Gospel Tabernacle, New York, Dr. Edward B. Shaw, of Monroe, N. Y., told of the lasting impression made upon him as a little boy in Hamilton when at the close of the first sermon he ever heard him preach, Dr. Simpson laid his hand in tender blessing on his head. He added that his mother so esteemed the young minister that she still inquires, 'Have you seen my pastor lately?' When I ask which pastor she means, her reply is 'I have only one pastor'."

Pastoral visitation was his delight, and so ardently did he pursue this and other service that we find the following minute under date of July 13, 1869. "That whereas our beloved pastor is suffering in health from the effects of close application to his ministerial duties, and feeling that cessation from work and change of scene may, by the divine blessing, prove beneficial to him, the session urgently requests him to rest for a period of two months and during that period to seek such scenes as may refresh his mind and be conducive to the restoration of his health." Mr. Simpson agreed to accept only one month of holiday.

Two years later he was granted four months' leave of absence for a visit to Europe, a trip he enjoyed to the full. His lecture on his observations abroad was brilliant and popular, but contrasts strangely with his accounts of his tours after the great awakening came into his life.

There are in it two passages which were almost prophetic of his later life. Here is one. "And here let us tread softly—we enter John Knox's house; we gaze on the interior as it was in the sixteenth century; we sit in his veritable study and very chair; and we inhale a fresh breath of his heroic spirit, so much needed in these weak times." How deeply the young Canadian preacher was to drink of that spirit he little dreamed that day.

He seemed to be moved even more deeply by his visit to the tomb of Sir Walter Scott. All of his own eloquence was fired by the memory of this noble Scotchman. Scott's struggle to meet enormous financial losses with his pen had caught the imagination and moved the heart that was later to pour itself out in books of more lasting value than *Waverley* and *Marmion*. He quotes: "I will dig in the mine of my imaginations for diamonds, or what may sell for diamonds, to meet all my engagements." What could better portray the closing days of his own life than this tender picture he gives us of Scott? "But, alas, nature sank in the unequal struggle, and the productions which the world enjoys today are the life-blood of a brave man's heart. His sun was largest at its setting; and though it went down among many clouds, it was a glorious sunset for a glorious soul, and sank, we trust, to shine in other climes in cloudless light."

A visitor to the manse on any Monday morning would have found the pastor occupied in the study with a group of fellow ministers. It was "blue Monday" in more senses than one, for some of them were addicted to the use of the weed. Sermons were discussed, and that facility for formulating outlines which amazed Dr. Simpson's students in later years was called into play in criticism of the past and prospective efforts of his friends.

Children's voices would be heard ringing through the house, for three sturdy boys and one little daughter came to bless their Canadian home. The firstborn was Albert

Henry, who was truly converted to God at an early age, but fell under temptation in New York City. His parents' prayers finally prevailed, and his last days were spent in devotedly assisting in his father's business affairs. "During his last illness, which continued over a year, the work of grace in his heart and life was most deeply marked and beautifully manifest. The crucible of suffering was used by the Heavenly Refiner to purify, soften, and sweeten his spirit, and at last the very light of heaven shone through the pale and suffering face and lighted up the crumbling temple with the glory of the life beyond." He entered into rest at thirty years of age.

The second child, Melville Jennings, was taken seriously ill with membraneous croup when only three and one-half years old while Mrs. Simpson was mourning the loss of her father in the old family home in Toronto. As his father carried him in his arms, just before his departure, he said, "Take me to Mamma," and when his mother appeared, he repeated to them the verse that she had taught him, "Abide in me and I in you." Mrs. Simpson says that this was the first message that ever sank deeply into her heart and that it prepared the way for the experience into which she entered years afterward.

The third boy, James Gordon Hamilton, was born on the 31st of August, 1870. Of him his father wrote: "In his early boyhood he gave his heart to the Lord and passed through a very distinct religious experience. In later years the temptations of city life frequently overcame him, and at times he wandered far from God. But it is a great comfort to his bereaved family and will be a source of joy to all his friends to know that in the last years of his life he was brought back by a very clear reli-

gious experience to his early faith, and after much suffering, borne with Christian patience, he entered into
rest at the age of thirty-seven with unclouded confidence
in the Saviour he had learned so tenderly to love and
trust."

The fourth child, Mabel, was also born in Hamilton.
On Feb. 11, 1891, she was united in marriage to Mr.
Hugh S. Brennen, a prominent business man of Hamilton, and a member of Knox Church. Both Mr. and Mrs.
Brennen were devoted Christians, and their home life
was ideal. Mr. Brennen was called home suddenly in
1912, leaving his wife and two daughters to prove the
all-sufficiency of the grace of our Lord and Saviour,
Jesus Christ.

The family circle was enlarged by the birth of another
daughter, Margaret May, in Louisville, and of the youngest boy, Howard Home, in New York City.

In 1894, when the congregation of Knox Church opened
their Sunday-school building, one of the finest at that
time in Canada, it happened to be the twenty-ninth anniversary of Dr. Simpson's ordination, and he was asked
to dedicate the building and to deliver several other addresses. The church could not hold the crowds that
thronged to hear him. He made this reference to the
occasion in *The Alliance Weekly:* "It was a most precious
token of our Father's love, after a generation of service,
that we should be able to come back to our earliest
friends, and find their hearts open, not only to us, but to
all the truth we brought them and, indeed, longing for a
deeper fullness of the Holy Spirit for their own life
and work."

On September 12, 1905, the fortieth anniversary of

his ordination, he revisited his first flock and was moved to write the following ordination hymn:

"Ordain me to Thy service, Lord;
    Baptize me with Thy power divine,
And help me for my future days
    To make my will entirely Thine.

"For twice a score of years Thy hand
    Has led Thy child along the way;
Oh, how Thy patient love has borne!
    Oh, how Thy grace has crowned each day!

"And if Thy mercy yet can trust
    A feeble worm to serve Thee still,
Ordain Thy child anew this day
    To better know and do Thy will.

"Correct my thoughts and let my life
    Speak louder than the words I say;
And give to me this joy supreme
    To know I please my Lord alway.

"Give me the very mind of Christ;
    Teach me to pray with power divine;
Baptize my lips with heavenly fire,
    And let my messages be Thine.

"And may the years Thou still mayest give
    Exalt my Lord and make Him known,
Till every land shall hear His Word
    And He can come to claim His own."

The most memorable visit was ten years later when he and Mrs. Simpson were asked to celebrate their jubilee with this beloved church which still delighted to honor him, though for thirty-five years he had not been in the Presbyterian ministry. He preached with unusual fervency, taking for the morning sermon the text used for his inaugural discourse fifty years before. In the evening he gave a clear statement of the truth and experience into which God had led him. On Monday a reception was given to Dr. and Mrs. Simpson, and the address which he then delivered showed that during his forty years' absence he had neither lost his love for Canada nor his facility as a lecturer.

Church minutes are usually dry reading, but Knox Church Session Minutes throw some strong sidelights on the results of his ministry. A great advance was made in the prayer life of the congregation by the institution of a social weekly prayer meeting in each elder's district, and later by establishing a united meeting for prayer at the close of the Wednesday evening lecture. The session also voted to discountenance the custom of holding funerals on the Sabbath. They departed so far from tradition as to grant the Sunday school permission to install a melodeon. Not the least interesting item is the resignation of an elder under discipline for intoxication.

A minute passed in response to questions from the General Assembly reveal how much progress has since been made in missionary interest. The session resolved: "That the missionary revenue of the church may be increased by the formation and vigorous operation of missionary associations ; in all the congregations of the Church, by the frequent diffusion of missionary intelligence, and by the establishment and successful working of a bona fide foreign mission in some heathen land, and we recommend China as at the present time the most promising opening for a new missionary enterprise."

The results of the nine years of ministry in Hamilton were extraordinary. No less than 750 members were received into church fellowship; a church debt of $8,000 was paid; contributions aggregating $50,000 were made, and during the last year the then unusual sum of $870 was given to missions, and $5,000 to other benevolences.

One of the Canadian delegates to the great Evangelical Alliance Conference in New York City in 1873 was A. B. Simpson. He was invited to preach for Dr. Burchard, in Thirteenth Street Presbyterian Church. In the audience were delegates from Chestnut Street Presbyterian Church, Louisville, Ky., who, on their return home, recommended this young Canadian to their congregation, which was without a pastor.

When the Presbytery of Hamilton met on December 3, 1873, there were before it calls to the pastor of Knox Church from Chalmers Church, Quebec, and Chestnut Street Church, Louisville, and a telegram had been received stating that commissioners were on their way with a call from Knox Church, Ottawa. Representatives of the session and the congregation of Knox Church were heard, who stated that with great reluctance they had agreed to release their beloved pastor if he himself should see his way clear to leave his charge. After several presbyters had spoken most appreciatively of his ministry it was agreed to grant the translation and to dissolve Mr. Simpson's pastoral connection with Knox Church on the twentieth day of December.

It was an affecting scene when the pastor bade farewell to his flock. The Ladies' Aid Association, which he had organized, presented him with an address, giving both him and Mrs. Simpson valuable tokens of remembrance. In his reply he gave thanks to God for His marvelous blessing on the work and to the people for their love and cooperation. The press, which had recognized his gifts by frequently publishing his addresses, expressed the regret felt in the city at the loss of such a brilliant preacher.   Before the year ended the family was speeding to its new home in the sunny South.

CHAPTER 6

PASTORAL EVANGELISM

CHESTNUT Street Church was the largest Presbyterian congregation in Louisville and the most influential in that synod of the Northern Presbyterian Church. It had noble traditions and challenged the best effort of the brilliant young Canadian who had been called to be its spiritual leader. An annual stipend of five thousand dollars relieved him of financial anxiety, and the welcome accorded to him and Mrs. Simpson promised well for a happy pastorate.

The inaugural sermon gave assurance of a true gospel ministry. It was a timely application of the text, "And they saw no man save Jesus only," leading up to a personal pledge and appeal to his people. "In coming among you, I am not ashamed to own this as the aim of my ministry and to take these words as the motto and keynote of my future preaching—Jesus only."

The young pastor was still treading the well-beaten paths of the modern church. How little he anticipated the developments that were to come in his life and ministry was shown by this sentence in his personal address to the congregation that morning: "I shall not prove to be the apostle of any new revelation or become the exponent of any new truth." New to him and to his flock were those revelations of the fullness of the Gospel which came when his own eyes had seen "no man save Jesus only." Strangely new would have sounded his great hymn, "Jesus Only," into which he compressed his later and richer conceptions, of which this is the refrain—

"Jesus only! Jesus ever!
  Jesus all in all we sing!
Saviour, Sanctifier, Healer,
  Glorious Lord and Coming King!"

It was not long till Louisville awakened to the fact that a very vital force had appeared. The city lay on the border line between the north and the south, and denominations had been divided on the question of slavery, some Louisville congregations adhering to one section and some to the other. A decade had not sufficed to reconcile brother to brother even within Christian circles. Mr. Simpson felt this hindrance keenly, and after much prayer, knowing that nothing would heal wounds like a revival, he invited all of the pastors of the city to meet in Chestnut Street Church to consult about bringing an evangelist for a series of union meetings. "But," said he, "we must have unity among ourselves first." They went to their knees and poured out their hearts for such a baptism of love as would sweep away their differences. When they rose, all but one were melted. At the second meeting two ministers who had not recognized each other since the war began shook hands.

This resulted in an evangelistic campaign conducted by one of the great evangelists of the day, Major Whittle, and that sweetest of gospel singers, P. P. Bliss. The city was stirred as never before, and hundreds were converted. How greatly Chestnut Street Church was quickened is shown by a report of the communion service which appeared in a daily paper.

"The building was filled to the utmost capacity, chairs and benches having been placed in the aisles and around the pulpit. Since the last communion season, three months ago, one hundred members have been added to the church, eighty-four having been received on profession of their faith in Jesus Christ as their Saviour since the beginning of the meetings conducted by Messrs. Whittle and Bliss. The pastor, Rev. A. B. Simpson, has labored with untiring patience and zeal, and has now the great joy of seeing this large number saved by the blood of the Lamb and safely sheltered within the fold on earth. His pastorate has been greatly blessed, and during the few months he has been with them one hundred and seventy-five have been added to the roll. He is faithful, tender, abundant in labors, and the work of the Lord is prospering in his hand."

Mr. Simpson was convinced that a united Sunday evening gospel meeting should be continued, and, failing to enlist the cooperation of the other churches, he determined to attempt it himself. Public Library Hall, where the revival meetings had been held, was engaged for these Sunday evening meetings, and the evening service in Chestnut Street Church was suspended. *The Courier-Journal* and other dailies gave unstinted support and defended him against unwarranted criticism. They published some of his addresses verbatim, and their wide constituency always received at least the heart of his message and an appreciative report of each meeting.

From the outset this unprecedented procedure on the part of a fashionable church met approval from the masses and was attended with divine blessing. Consequently, what began as an experiment continued as an "institution." In the late spring, a reporter wrote:

"Public Library Hall, seating more than two thousand, has been filled to overflowing with the representatives of all classes of society. Mr. Simpson's forte is pathos; his pungent deductions, lucid illustrations, and incisive appeals are but so many strands of a pathetic line of discourse that breaks down, oftentimes, the sturdiest indifference, takes sophistry by storm, and vitalizes the most dormant resolution." Another reporter says that, "He broke through the barriers of the pulpit, dissipated the reserve of a professional divine, and talked as one young man talking to another. The effect of this was, what Mr. Simpson himself may not have noticed particularly, that in the ensuing days every one who had heard him and who chanced to meet him saluted him as an acquaintance."

The singing of P. P. Bliss convinced Mr. Simpson of the wisdom of giving a large place to the ministry of song, and in all his subsequent work, not only chorus and congregational singing, but solos were special features. He was a keen critic of the work of the soloist and was satisfied with nothing less than a musical message given with the same motive and spirit in which he preached. Mr. Bliss returned more than once to sing in the Sunday night meetings, and his tragic death in a railway accident was a great blow to Mr. Simpson. The regular soloist, Mr. D. McPherson, was an effective co-worker throughout the Louisville meetings.

The winter campaign was so successful that Mr. Simpson proposed to model the future work of the church on this pattern, and to this end suggested the erection of a tabernacle in a central location on Broadway, a short distance from the old church. The congregation concurred, purchased a suitable site on the corner of Broadway and Fourth Avenue, and proceeded to build their new home. A conservative minority opposed this and withdrew, forming the nucleus of another church.

The Sunday night service was resumed in the fall of

1875. It seems that subtle opposition prevented the use of Public Library Hall, and consequently Macauley's Theatre was engaged. This led to another storm of criticism on the part of a certain element in the churches, and caustically censorious articles on "Sunday Theatricals" appeared in a religious journal. The *Kentucky Presbyterian* defended the course taken, and the city papers were, if possible, more cordial in their support than during the previous winter. Even larger numbers attended than during the former season, and frequently many could not gain admittance. It was not uncommon to hold an after meeting for which many remained. During that winter hundreds confessed Christ as their Saviour.

The tabernacle was not opened till June 9, 1878, nearly three years after it was undertaken. The original estimates called for an outlay of $65,000, all of which was subscribed, but, contrary to the pastor's wishes, the plans had been altered and the completed structure cost $105,000. With a seating capacity of more than two thousand, the auditorium combined simplicity, beauty, and perfect acoustic effect, while in its external architecture it was one of the most imposing churches west of New York City. But the debt hung like a cloud on Mr. Simpson's spirit and, at the dedicatory service, he poured out his soul in a burning and almost pathetic plea to the congregation.

"Side by side with other churches, with a definite denominational basis and a broad and liberal spirit, we desire as our specific aim, besides the great work of edifying the Church and sending the Gospel to the world, to draw to this house, and through it to the cross and the Saviour, the great masses of every social condition who attend no church and practically know no God. It will expose us to just criticism if we have built a home we cannot afford to own. It will prove a fetter to our freedom and our energies. Church debts are properly called *church bonds*.

"There are two things this church must be if it is to be blessed. One is, *it must be free,* free in the full sense that all shall give gladly, freely to God according to their means—the cents of the poor being as welcome as the thousands of the rich—and no poor man excluded because the rich can pay $100 per year for a pew. But a church with a debt can never do this satisfactorily. The other is *it must be unselfish and missionary.* If this Tabernacle is not able to give up every year as much to the great cause of the conversion of the world as to its own support, it stands as a living embodiment of selfishness and will die of chills. Now a church with bonds cannot be a successful missionary church. Every call for the conversion of the world will be answered by the low, sullen word—debt . . . And therefore the easiest way would be to make one brave, final sacrifice . . . This morning I desire to place on this pulpit the simple standard, *Broadway Tabernacle Free!* free from debt, free to God, free to all."

On that Sabbath morning a throng of nearly three thousand people saw the strange spectacle of a formal opening of a church without a dedication. The pastor's appeal had failed, and he refused to dedicate to God a building that was mortgaged. For two years he preached in it; and when he resigned, it was still mortgaged and undedicated.

Years afterward Mr. Simpson wrote: "Unable to get my people to pray about it, I prayed myself and claimed it of God in absolute, implicit faith. One year and a half after I came to New York I received one morning a telegram in these words: 'Tabernacle debt paid yesterday. Come next Sabbath and dedicate it. Bring Mrs. Simpson with you.' Of course we went, and the most wonderful thing about it was that the elder who regarded my prayer as impracticable gave $40,000 of the whole amount and was one of the first to receive us to the hospitality of his home as his guests."

At its dedication the name of the church was changed from Broadway Tabernacle to Warren Memorial, in honor of Mr. L. L. Warren, who had been instrumental in freeing it from debt. Two months afterwards it was destroyed by fire, but "rose, phoenix-like from its ruin, and stands today as a monument to its founder."

Robert Lowe Fletcher writes with keen insight of this period of Mr. Simpson's life. "It was in 1876 I heard him for the first time, became associated with him in religious work, and a member of his flock . . . The details of his ministry possibly are most valuable and interesting as showing the leadings of the Holy Spirit in preparing a man for a great work—faith tried by fire . . . While his was not then the Spirit-filled life it afterward became, it was nevertheless characterized by zeal for souls and intensity of purpose of the Pauline type—such as mocked the cross and flame in the direst period of primal church history. But the rare enduement and endowment of intellectual gifts and graces were ever too conspicuous to escape the favorable attention of the most casual observer. At that time, his modest, shrinking nature would have forbade his entertaining such high hopes for his ministry as were realized, for to the very last he cared not that the world should hear of him but *his mes-*

sage. Nevertheless, those, who like myself were privileged to form direct impressions, recognized in that formative period of a divinely appointed career a latent power, as here and there was a sparkling radiance in his pulpit oratory that was to be notable, under God, for efficiency and power."

One of his most distinguished fellow students, Dr. J. Munroe Gibson, of London, England, says in a recent letter:

"Since our student days I remember only one occasion on which I met him. It was in Louisville and must have been between '76 and '80. I thought, 'There is a man who must have made marvelous progress since the old student days,' and I felt rebuked in his presence. He now struck me as a man of mark, and what is much more, a man of God."

Mr. Simpson's pastoral work in Louisville was quite as extraordinary as his pulpit ministry. On one occasion he was impelled to call upon a prominent citizen very late at night. It seemed the more unreasonable because a fierce storm was raging, but he finally yielded to the impulse. The gentleman was surprised, but invited him into his study; and when he learned that concern for his eternal welfare, about which he himself took little thought, had brought the pastor out at such an unseemly time, he was convicted and turned to the Lord.

There was a young man among the converts who was so earnestly seeking to follow the Lord that he secured the pastor's consent to spend half of his lunch hour with him daily, and under this influence seemed to be gaining strength and overcoming his temptations. When informed on one occasion that the pastor would be out of the city for a few days, his face fell. Then Mr. Simpson said,

"Will, how would it be, if instead of spending a half hour with you daily, I could live in you?" "Oh, that would be fine," Will replied, "for then I should always think and do and say just what you would." "Then why not believe that Jesus Himself lives in you, Will?" said his pastor. When Mr. Simpson returned, Will did not come as usual at the noontime; so he went to see what was the matter. Will greeted him with a happy face and said, "Pastor, it works. I shall not need to trouble you now, for I have found that Christ really lives in me."

Another incident, which he narrates in *Messages of Love,* shows how he enlisted the service of his flock. "I found in the outskirts of the city one of our neglected poor so ignorant of human love that she could not comprehend at first what I meant when I told her of the love of God. She had been neglected, abused, and wronged so long that her hand was against every man, and every man's hand was against her. When I tried to lead her to the knowledge of Jesus, she looked up into my face and said, "I do not understand you; nobody ever loved me, and I do not even know what love means." I went home that night to my proud and wealthy church, and I told them I wanted them to make a poor sister understand the meaning of love. And so they began one by one to visit her, to give her little tokens of their interest and regard; until at last one day, months later, as I sat in her humble room, she looked up in my face and said with much feeling, 'Now I think I understand what love means, and can accept the love of God'."

In one of the last lectures he delivered to the students at Nyack he gave another experience from this period.

"I remember spending a whole month in the early part of my Christian experience in seeking a blessing. On the first day of the new year I started to wait on God for a wonderful baptism. I said, 'I shall spend this week and set it apart, shutting myself away from everybody.' I went home occasionally to my meals, but dropped my visiting and pastoral work and just spent the time on my face before the Lord. The Lord met me, of course, but I did not feel satisfied at the end of the week. I was less satisfied at the end of the second; at the end of the third I began to have the strangest sensations, and at the end of the fourth week I was nearly crazy. I said, 'Lord, why don't You meet me? What is the matter?' and at last in desperation I opened my Bible and said, 'Show me what You want to say to me.' In the last chapter of Matthew I found the words, 'He is not here; he is risen; he goeth before you into Galilee; there shall ye see him.' In that moment I remembered there were a lot of sick people I had not visited for four weeks, and others in desperate need. I hurried up the street to the first home, where lay a suffering one whom I had not visited for some time. I had not prayed two sentences until the heavens opened, and I had a wonderful baptism of the Holy Ghost. I found Him when I took Him by faith and went forward to use Him and turn my blessing into a blessing for some one else."

The story of Mr. Simpson's new revelation of Christ, of his physical collapse, of the growing missionary vision, and other threads interwoven in the Louisville ministry is part of later chapters. On November 7, 1879, after almost six years of strenuous service, he resigned to accept a call to a larger field and to new experiences.

CHAPTER 7

THE LIFE CRISIS

THE life of A. B. Simpson can never be interpreted correctly if the great crisis through which he passed, after he had been in the ministry for more than ten years, is not thoroughly understood. This was not only the beginning of his larger life and ministry, but it also changed his whole view of the Christian life and deeply colored all his after teaching. Moreover, it led him into the rugged, lonely path which they must tread who wholly follow the Lord. "I have lived a lonely life" was one of his last personal remarks to the Nyack students. He tasted, as few have done, at once of the bitterness of separation from friends and former associates who did not follow with him in his new-found path, and of the sweetness of fellowship with those who were one with him in spirit and aim.

Addressing a sympathetic audience in London, he said, "Well do I remember when first the Holy Ghost came into my heart, how lonely I felt, how far I was removed from my old Christian associates—they could not understand me; but when I found one or two who did understand me, how dear they became to me! They were more than brothers, more than sisters. We could get closer because we could get deeper and higher in God's way. Then I remember how, when I got a little further and found that this blessed Jesus is a living Christ, that not only is His spirit for my spirit, but His body for my body, touching mine into life, and holding and quickening it with His own resurrection life—then again I felt so lonesome. My old friends seemed to leave me, and for months I seemed to be alone, separated from hundreds and thousands of ministers and people I had loved and worked with all my life. But when one and two and three began to come and join this little band, oh, how much deeper was the bond of love!"

On the same occasion he gave this simple statement regarding three experiences which mark the great epochs in his life. "Some twenty-seven years ago, I floundered for ten months in the waters of despondency, and I got out of them just by believing in Jesus as my Saviour. About twelve years ago I got into another deep experience of conviction, and I got out of that by believing in Jesus as my Sanctifier. After years of teaching from and waiting on Him, the Lord Jesus Christ showed me four years ago that it was His blessed will to be my complete Saviour for body as well as soul."

The first of these experiences has been narrated in Dr. Simpson's reminiscences. He entered into a deep and abiding sense of "peace with God through our Lord Jesus Christ." He lived and ministered in this precious revelation, preaching justification as taught in the fifth chapter of Romans, with great power and unction. Of the truth declared in the sixth chapter he had then no personal experience, while of the heights and depths of the eighth chapter he had but glimpses. His personal experience was the conflict so vividly described in the seventh chapter of that epistle.

In a sermon to his first congregation in Hamilton on the fiftieth anniversary of his ordination, he made humble reference to this condition. "Fifty years ago the one who addresses you this evening was ordained in this sacred place. He was a young, ambitious minister of twenty-one and had not yet learned the humbling lessons which God in faithful love is pleased to teach us as fast as we are willing to learn. He was sincere and earnest up to the light that he had received, but even after the nine years of active ministry in Hamilton he had not yet learned the deeper lessons of spiritual life and power which God was pleased to open to him after taking him from this place. There is a remarkable passage in Isaiah telling us that when the Spirit is poured out from on high, the wilderness shall become a fruitful field, and the fruitful field shall be counted for a forest. When that experience came to him, the field of his former ministry, which had been so fruitful, suddenly appeared barren and withered, and he felt that his true ministry had scarcely yet begun."

The second great crisis began early in his Louisville ministry. Contact with those Spirit-filled evangelists, Whittle and Bliss, awakened him to his lack of spiritual power for life and service and led him to seek the infilling of the Holy Spirit.

He has left us this clear-cut testimony about this crisis. "I look back with unutterable gratitude to the lonely and sorrowful night when, mistaken in many things and imperfect in all, and not knowing but that it would be death in the most literal sense before the morning light, my heart's first full consecration was made, and with unreserved surrender I first could say,

> 'Jesus, I my cross have taken,
> All to leave and follow Thee;
> Destitute, despised, forsaken,
> Thou from hence my All shall be.'

Never, perhaps, has my heart known quite such a thrill

of joy as when the following Sabbath morning I gave
out those lines and sang them with all my heart. And
if God has been pleased to make my life in any measure a
little temple for His indwelling and for His glory, and
if He ever shall be pleased to use me in any fuller measure, it has been because of that hour, and it will be still
in the measure in which that hour is made the key-note
of a consecrated, crucified, and Christ-devoted life."

His experience, as well as his close study of the Word,
convinced him that many refuse the workings of the Holy
Spirit as He seeks to lead them through such a crisis into
the fullness of God. The pathos of it moved him when
he wrote,

> "They came to the gates of Canaan,
>   But they never entered in;
> They came to the very threshold,
>   But they perished in their sin."

All this was to him both a new theory and a new experience. "I used to think," he says, "that we were sanctified at last in order to get to heaven—that the very
last thing God did for the soul was to sanctify it, and
that then He took it right home; and I will confess that
at that time I was a good deal afraid of being sanctified
for fear I should die very soon afterward. But the Lord
Jesus Christ tells us that we are sanctified in order to
serve Him here."

Step by step he learned the true meaning of a sanctified
life. Commenting on Psalm 110, he says, "Consecration
must come first and then sanctification. We can conse-
crate ourselves as freewill offerings; then God sanctifies
us and clothes us with the beauties of His holiness. The
consecration is ours; the sanctification is His."

In a brief exposition of the Fourfold Gospel he writes

of the definiteness of this crisis in unequivocal terms. "We also believe, and this is the emphatic point in our testimony, that this experience of Christ our Sanctifier marks a definite and distinct crisis in the history of a soul. We do not grow into it, but we cross a definite line of demarcation as clear as when the hosts of Joshua crossed the Jordan and were over in the promised land and set up a great heap of stones so that they never could forget that crisis hour."

Dr. Simpson regarded the Holy Spirit as the divine agent in this blessed experience of sanctification. "Therefore the baptism of the Holy Spirit is simultaneous with our union with the Lord Jesus; the Spirit does not act apart from Christ, but it is His to take of the things of Christ and show them unto us."

In the *Fullness of Jesus* he states this in another way. "The indwelling of the Holy Ghost in the human spirit is quite distinct from the work of regeneration. In Ezekiel 36:26 they are most clearly distinguished. The one is described as the taking away of 'the stony heart' and giving 'an heart of flesh'; of the other it is said: 'I will put my spirit within you, and cause you to walk in my statutes, and ye shall keep my judgments and do them.' The one is like the building of the house; the other the owner moving in and making it his own personal residence."

In a passage from *The Christ of the Forty Days* we read: "There is a great difference between our receiving power from the Holy Ghost and our receiving the Holy Ghost as our power. In the latter case we are as insignificant and insufficient as ever, and it is the Person who dwells within us who possesses and exercises all the gifts and powers of our ministry, and only as we abide in Him and He works in us are we able to exercise this power."

He learned, too, that "what men and women need to know to-day is not sanctification as a state, but Christ as a living Person." In his much quoted tract *Himself*, we find him saying, "I prayed a long time to get sanctified, and sometimes I thought I had it. On one occasion I felt something, and I held on with a desperate grip for fear I should lose it, and kept awake the whole night fearing it would go. And, of course, it went with the next sensation and the next mood. Of course I lost *it* because I did not hold on to Him." Out of such painful experience grew his glad song:

> "Once it was the blessing,
>   Now it is the Lord;
> Once it was the feeling,
>   Now it is His Word;
> Once His gift I wanted,
>   Now, the Giver own;
> Once I sought for healing,
>   Now Himself alone."

This became so clear to him that he never preached *perfection* but a perfect Christ abiding in the sanctified believer. He taught that "sanctification is divine holiness, not human self improvement, nor perfection. It is the inflow into man's being of the life and purity of His own perfection and the working out of His own will."

Dr. Simpson believed that this is *"complete,* but not *completed; perfect,* but not *perfected.* He states this admirably in *Wholly Sanctified.* "He is the Author and Finisher of our faith, and the true attitude of the consecrated heart is that of a constant yielding and constant receiving. This last view of sanctification gives boundless scope to our spiritual progress. It is here that the gradual phase of sanctification comes in. Commencing with a complete separation from evil and dedication to God, it now advances into all the fullness of Christ, and grows up to the measure of the stature of perfect manhood in Him, until every part of our being and every part of our life is filled with God and becomes a channel to receive, and a medium to reflect His grace and glory."

A close study of Dr. Simpson's life in Louisville reveals that the fullness of these great truths did not burst upon him suddenly. The great crisis moment came in 1874, but it was not until the summer of 1881 that he entered into the rest that remaineth for the people of God, thenceforth to live and work in continual consciousness of the all-sufficiency of Christ for spirit, soul, and body.

It was a stern school through which the Lord led him. He recalls that "In a crisis hour of my spiritual experience while asking counsel from an old, experienced friend, I was shocked to receive this answer, 'All you need in order to bring you into the blessing you are seeking, and to make your life a power for God, is to be annihilated.' The fact is the shock of that message almost annihilated me for the time, but before God's faithful discipline was through, I had learned in some adequate measure, as I have been learning ever since, the great truth. that I am not sufficient to think anything of myself." Herein he was finding companionship with Moses, for in *Divine Emblems* he writes, "When God gets him there, reduced to the smallest of proportions, the weakest of all men that ever lived, He says, 'You are ready for work; now, Moses, I am going to take that rod and with it break the arms of Pharaoh and open the way for My people, and bring waters from the desert rock, and make you an instrument of power'"

Another incident, which he sometimes referred to, shows how he entered into another phase of this life. "Many years ago, the life of the great Hildebrand became an inspiration to me, especially when I learned that he had chosen a patron saint as the guardian of his life, and attributed all his success to the care of St. Peter, to whom he had devoted his life. Blessed be God, there is a greater than he! and when I read the story, I said, 'I, too, shall choose a patron saint.' But it was none other than the blessed Son of God; and thanks to His dear name, whatever I have known of strength for soul and body, of blessing in the Master's service, it has been through His care and friendship. In some little measure I can say,

> 'Jesus, Jesus, how I trust Thee,
>   How I've proved Thee o'er and o'er;
> Jesus, Jesus, precious Jesus,
>   Oh, for grace to trust Thee more'."

How intense was his spiritual longing in those days and how wonderfully the Spirit of God guided him to the great central truth of which he was to become a special exponent is shown in the following narrative. "Once in my early ministry I travelled a thousand miles to go to one of Mr. Moody's conventions of ministers in Chicago. I reached there about six o'clock in the evening and went up to the early meeting. I did not hear Mr. Moody say anything, but one plain, earnest preacher got up with his face all shining. He said, 'I came up here expecting Mr. Moody to help me. But last night I saw Jesus, and I got such a look at Jesus that I am never going to need anything again as long as I live.' And he wound up with a long Hallelujah. Something smote my heart. 'All you need is Jesus; you go to Him.' I took the train back home that night. I did not wait for the convention. I went to my office in the church vestry, and I waited there on my face at His blessed feet until He came, and thank God, He enabled me in some measure to say,

> I have seen Jesus, and my heart is dead to all beside;
> I have seen Jesus, and my wants are all supplied;
> I have seen Jesus, and my heart is satisfied,
>   Satisfied with Jesus."

One of the lessons came through his failure to lead his loved flock with him in these new-found pastures. They had gloried in his evangelical preaching and had taken the unprecedented action of following him from their comfortable church home to a public hall in order to reach the unchurched masses. But they halted half way on the path of sacrifice and ended in erecting a magnificent modern church loaded with debt, thus defeating his purpose. Nor had they any sympathy with his strong stand in declining to accept a salary as long as they refused to discharge the mortgage. It weighed upon his sensitive spirit, and this even more than his unceasing labors resulted in a collapse so serious that for a time it seemed that his ministry was ended. Then it was that a larger ministry unfolded before him, and "the uttermost part of the earth" became his objective.

The third great crisis to which he refers followed another collapse when he was so broken that the help of man was unavailing. Then he found that one of the provisions of redemption is "that the life also of Jesus might be made manifest in our body," and that by this same redemption right "we have the mind of Christ." How this came about he himself will now tell us.

CHAPTER 8

DIVINE LIFE FOR THE BODY

I T was while Mr. Simpson was pastor of the Thirteenth Street Presbyterian Church in New York that he found the secret of divine life for the body and entered into an experience of physical healing, which bore him through thirty-five years of the most strenuous toil in a way which caused multitudes to marvel.

Some years before, during his pastorate in Louisville, he had been deeply impressed by the healing of a young paralytic in his congregation. He thus describes the effect upon himself:

"The impression produced by this incident never left my heart. Soon afterwards I attempted to take the Lord as my Healer, and for a while, as long as I trusted Him, He sustained me wonderfully; but afterwards, being entirely without instruction, and advised by a devout Christian physician that it was presumption, I abandoned my position of simple dependence upon God alone, and so floundered and stumbled for years. But as I heard of isolated cases, I never desired to doubt them or question that God did sometimes so heal. For myself, however, the truth had no really practical or effectual power, for I never could feel that I had any clear authority in a given case of need to trust myself to Him."

This experience is no extraordinary one. Thousands of devout servants of God are living as he then lived, some of whom are unwise enough to assert that there is nothing better promised us in the Bible, during this dispensation at least. For such Mr. Simpson had great sympathy, for he knew that the Holy Spirit alone ever led him to see that he had a right to the life of Christ for body, mind and spirit.

In *The Gospel of Healing,* a little book which he wrote nearly thirty years ago, and which has been issued in many editions, there is a chapter in which he tells how he was led to see and accept the truth of divine healing. Among his papers was a revision of this personal testimony, intended for a new edition which was about to be published. As this is his life-long, as well as his latest testimony, we shall let him tell the story.

"For more than twenty years I was a sufferer from many physical infirmities and disabilities. Beginning a life of hard study, at the age of fourteen I broke down hopelessly with nervous prostration while I was preparing for college, and for many months was not permitted by my physician even to look at a book. During this time I came very near death, and on the verge of eternity gave myself to God. After my college studies were completed, I became the ambitious pastor of a large city church at twenty-one, and plunging headlong into my work, I again broke down with heart trouble and had to go away for months of rest, returning at length, as it seemed to me at the time, to die. Rallying, however, and slowly recovering in part, I labored on for years with the aid of constant remedies and preventives. I carried a bottle of ammonia in my pocket for years, and would have taken a nervous spasm if I had ventured without it. Again and again, while climbing a slight elevation or going up a stair did the old suffocating agony come over me. God knows how many hundred times in my earlier ministry when preaching in my pulpit or ministering by a grave it seemed that I must fall in the midst of the service or drop into that open grave.

"Two other collapses of long duration came in my health, and again and again during these terrible seasons did it seem that the last drops of life were ebbing out, and a frail thread held the vital chain from snapping forever.

"A few months before I took Christ as my Healer, a prominent physician in New York told me that I had not constitutional strength enough left to last more than a few months.

"During the summer that followed I went for a time to Saratoga Springs, and while there, one Sabbath afternoon, I wandered out to the Indian camp ground, where the jubilee singers were leading the music in an evangelistic service. I was deeply depressed, and all things in life looked dark and withered. Suddenly, I heard the chorus:

> 'My Jesus is the Lord of lords:
> No man can work like Him.'

"Again and again, in the deep bass notes, and the higher tones that seemed to soar to heaven, they sang:

> 'No man can work like Him,
> No man can work like Him.'

"It fell upon me like a spell. It fascinated me. It seemed like a voice from heaven. It possessed my whole being. I took Him also to be *my* Lord of lords, and to work for *me*. I knew not how much it all meant; but I took Him in the dark, and went forth from that old-fashioned service, remembering nothing else, but strangely lifted up.

"A few weeks later I went with my family to Old

Orchard Beach, Me., chiefly to enjoy the delightful air of that loveliest of all ocean beaches. I lived on the seashore while there, and went occasionally to the meetings on the camp ground, but only once or twice took part in them, and had not, up to that time, committed myself in any full sense to the truth or experience of divine healing. I heard a great number of people testify that they had been healed by simply trusting the Word of Christ, just as they would for salvation. It drove me to my Bible. I determined that I must settle this matter one way or the other. I am so glad I did not go to man. At His feet, alone, with my Bible open, and with no one to help or guide me, I became convinced that this was part of Christ's glorious Gospel for a sinful and suffering world, for all who would believe and receive His Word.

"That was enough. I could not believe this and then refuse to take it for myself, for I felt that I dare not hold any truth in God's Word as a mere theory or teach to others what I had not personally proved. And so one Friday afternoon at the hour of three o'clock, I went out into the silent pine woods—I remember the very spot—and there I raised my right hand to heaven and made to God, as if I had seen Him there before me face to face, these three great and eternal pledges:

"1. As I shall meet Thee in that day, I solemnly accept this truth as part of Thy Word and of the Gospel of Christ, and, God helping me, I shall never question it until I meet Thee there.

"2. As I shall meet Thee in that day, I take the Lord Jesus as my physical life, for all the needs of my body until all my lifework is done; and, God helping me, I shall never doubt that He does become my life and strength from this moment and will keep me under all circumstances until all His will for me is perfectly fulfilled.

"3. As I shall meet Thee in that day, I solemnly promise *to use* this blessing for the glory of God and the good of others, and to so speak of it or minister in connection with it in any way in which God may call me or others may need me in the future.

"I arose. It had only been a few moments, but I knew that something was done. Every fibre of my soul was tingling with a sense of God's presence. I do not know whether my body felt better or not—I know I did not think of it—it was so glorious to believe it simply, and to know that henceforth He had it in hand.

"Then came the test of faith. The first struck me before I had left the spot. A subtle voice whispered: 'Now you have decided to take God as your Healer, it would help if you should just go down to Dr. Cullis' cottage and get him to pray with you.' I listened to it for a moment. The next moment a blow seemed to strike my brain, which made me reel as a man stunned. I cried: 'Lord, what have I done?' I felt I was in some great peril. In a moment the thought came very quickly: 'That suggestion would have been all right before this, but you have just settled this matter forever, and told God that you will never doubt that it is done, and you must not attempt to do it over again.' I saw it like a flash of lightning, and in that moment I understood what faith meant and what a solemn thing it was inexorably to keep faith with God. I have often thanked God for that blow. I saw that when a thing was settled with God, it was never to be unsettled or repeated. When it was done, it was never to be undone or done over again in any sense that could involve a doubt of the finality of the committal already made. I think in the early days of the work of faith to which God afterwards called me, I was as much helped by a holy fear of doubting God as by any of the joys and raptures of His presence or promises. This little word often shone like a living fire in my Bible: 'If any man draw back, my soul shall have no pleasure in him.' What the enemy desired was to get some doubt about the certainty and completeness of the transaction just closed, and God mercifully held me back from it.

"The day after I started to the mountains of New Hampshire. The next test came on the following Sabbath, just two days after I had claimed my healing. I was invited to preach in the Congregational Church. I felt the Holy Spirit pressing me to give a special testimony. But I tried to preach a good sermon of my own choosing. It was about the Holy Ghost, and had often been blessed, but it was not His word for that hour, I am sure. He wanted me to tell the people what He had been showing me. But I tried to be conventional and respectable, and I had an awful time. My jaws seemed like lumps of lead, and my lips would scarcely move. I got through as soon as I could, and fled into an adjoining field, where I lay before the Lord and asked Him to show me what my burden meant and to forgive me. He did.most graciously, and let me have one more chance to testify for Him and glorify Him. That night we had a service in our hotel, and I was permitted to speak again. This time I did tell what God had been doing. Not very much did I say, but I tried to be faithful in a stammering way, and told the people how I had lately seen the Lord Jesus in a deeper fullness, as the Healer of the body, and had taken Him for myself, and knew that He would be

faithful and sufficient. God did not ask me to testify of
my feelings or experiences, but of Jesus and His faithfulness. And I am sure He calls all who trust Him to testify before they experience His full blessing. I believe I
should have lost my healing if I had waited until I
felt it.

"Well, the next day the third test came. Near by was
a mountain 3,000 feet high; I was asked to join a little
party that was to ascend it. I shrank back at once. Did
I not remember the dread of high altitudes that had always overshadowed me, and the terror with which I had
resolved in Switzerland and Florence never to attempt it
again?

"Then came the solemn searching thought, 'If you fear
to go, it is because you do not believe that God has
healed you. If you have taken Him for your strength,
need you fear to do anything to which He calls you?'

"I felt it was God's thought. I felt my fear would be,
in this case, pure unbelief, and I told God that in His
strength I would go.

"And so I ascended that mountain. At first it seemed
as if it would take my last breath. I felt all the old
weakness and dread; I found I had in myself no more
strength than ever. But over against my weakness and
suffering I became conscious that there was another
Presence. There was a divine strength reached out to
me if I would take it, claim it, hold it, and persevere in it.
When I reached the mountain top, I seemed to be at
the gate of heaven, and the world of weakness and fear
was lying at my feet. Thank God, from that time I have
had a new heart in this breast, literally as well as spiritually, and Christ has been its glorious life.

"The Lord has often permitted the test to be a very

severe one. A few months after my healing He called
me into the special pastoral, literary and missionary work
which has since engaged my time and energy, and which
has involved much more labor than any previous period
of my life. And yet I desire to record my testimony to
the honor and glory of Christ, that it has been a continual
delight and much easier in every way than the far lighter
tasks of former years. I have been conscious, however,
all the time that I was not using my own natural strength.
Physically I do not think I am any more robust than ever.
I am intensely conscious with every breath, that I am
drawing my vitality from a directly supernatural source,
and that it keeps pace with the calls and necessities of
my work. I believe and am sure that it is nothing else
than the life of Christ manifested in my mortal flesh. I
do not desire to provoke argument, but I give my simple,
humble testimony, and to me it is very real and very wonderful. I know 'it is the Lord'."

The idea is too common that a person who is healed is
thereafter immune from every kind of sickness. Dr.
Simpson's conception of divine life for the body was
exactly contrary to this supposition. He felt himself to
be wholly dependent upon a vital and continuous connection with the Lord for his life.

He illustrated this by a personal incident. One night
he found it necessary to search for some papers in an
office which he had abandoned, from which all lighting
and heating appliances had been removed. There was a
heap of ashes in the grate and a large bottle of oil on
the mantel. It occurred to him to pour the oil upon the
ashes, and the light and heat thus supplied enabled him
to accomplish his purpose. He says: "It was a beautiful
parable to me. There was a time when my physical

strength, like that heap of ashes, was burned out, but
lo! I found a vessel of oil, the blessed Holy Ghost, and
as God poured His fullness on my exhausted frame, a
divine strength came, full of sweet exhilaration and un-
wearied buoyancy and energy, and in that light and life
of God I am working without exhaustion, and trust still
to work in His glorious all-sufficiency until my work is
done."

A definite instance in which this simple secret of life
was manifested is narrated by Rev. W. T. MacArthur.
"Mr. Simpson had contracted a heavy cold, and was
really a sick man, but he delivered the convention address
for which he had come to Chicago. At the close of the
meeting I accompanied him to his hotel where he sat for
a few minutes in the lobby. He was breathing heavily
and ablaze with fever. I said, 'Mr. Simpson, is there
nothing I can do for you?' He replied, 'Yes, Mr. Mac-
Arthur, you can say good night. I must be alone with
God.' Early in the morning I called him by telephone.
I should not have been greatly astonished if there had
been no response. However, the signal had no sooner
been given than I heard his voice sharp and clear. He
seemed surprised that I should be enquiring for his
health, and asked me kindly if *I* had rested well. He was
just leaving for a convention four hundred miles farther
west. I also was to speak at that convention, and arrived there about twenty-four hours after he did. All
agreed that they had never seen him looking better, and
had never heard him preach so well."

Some years ago Dr. Simpson himself told the Nyack
students of one of his many experiences. He had been
hastening down the hill from his home to catch the early
morning train when he slipped and dislocated his knee-

cap. The pain was intense, and he was unable to stand. "Sitting there on the ice," he said, "I held my knee up and silently prayed, when suddenly it seemed as if the very love of the Lord was bathing it and the pain turned into an exquisite sensation that seemed like a physical joy."

It seems not a little strange that we should expect those who trust the Lord for their bodies to manifest continually a perfect physical life while, at the same time, we excuse ourselves and others for very evident failures in spiritual life. The Apostle John expressed his ardent wish for his friends in this prayer: "Beloved, I wish above all things that thou mayest prosper and be in health, even as thy soul prospereth." Dr. Simpson believed that this was the true measure of divine life for the body, for to him body, soul, and spirit were inseparably related and each equally provided for in the dispensation of divine grace.

Some have thought that Dr. Simpson changed his views and attitude in his later years. Nothing could be further from the truth. Those who knew him most intimately all bear witness to his unshaken confidence in the Lord as the Healer of His people. Even when he himself in his last days was not restored, as he earnestly prayed that he would be, his faith did not for a moment fail. He had never attempted, as some have done, to explain some of the mysteries that sorely perplex those who demand that the secrets of the individual soul in its relationship to God shall be understood by others. We shall do well to be as wise as he was in leaving some things to be made manifest when we shall "know as also we are known," and even to be willing to allow God to keep some of His own secrets.

CHAPTER 9

IN THE GREAT METROPOLIS

THE providences of God were most manifest in Dr. Simpson's call to New York City. His ministry in Louisville had been not only successful, but had marked an epoch in his life. It had been as much of a training school to God's servant as a ministry to God's people. He was ready for a new departure in life and service, and it was doubtful if his flock would follow their shepherd into these new pastures. Yet another man with ideals in consonance with theirs would find an exceedingly inviting prospect in the pastorate.

On the other hand, Dr. Simpson was coveted as the successor of his old friend, Dr. Burchard. It was in this pulpit that the Louisville elders had heard him preach before they recommended him to their congregation. It is said that on the occasion of one visit his message had so impressed the people and the pastor that Dr. Burchard would not speak from the pulpit for some time afterward, but addressed his flock from the floor.

New York City presented an unlimited field for such work as had been attempted in Louisville if only forces could be released to conduct it. The conviction of a call to such work was deeper than ever, nor was this young pastor yet prepared to admit that it could not be done in and through a regular church channel.

The call to the unevangelized did not come merely from a city, however great and needy. The "man of Macedonia" had beckoned the Canadian schoolboy to the

South Seas, and in Louisville he had heard the same clamant call from China.   In New York he would be at the missionary center of his own denomination and others, and plans were formulating for a personal ministry on behalf of the Christless millions.

All of these considerations and others weighed with Mr. Simpson in accepting the call from the Thirteenth Street Presbyterian Church of New York City in November, 1879.   His first discourse, on Acts 1:7, 8, left no doubt that he had come among them to declare the Gospel in dependence upon the Holy Spirit.   In the second week of January, 1880, a periodical reported that "As a result of a deep and growing work of grace which has manifested itself for several weeks, thirty-seven persons were welcomed into communion, twenty of whom were received on profession of faith.   The attendance on the Sabbath and at the usual week services has largely increased.   During the Week of Prayer meetings were held every evening, and are being continued this week. The people of God are greatly revived and strengthened, and many of the unconverted are seeking Jesus Christ and His salvation."   This revival spirit continued, and the warm-hearted pastoral ministrations, combined with unusual preaching, greatly endeared him to the congregation, the surviving members of which still hold him in the highest esteem.

It is needless to say that no success within the limits of a church building and congregation, however marked, could have satisfied Mr. Simpson at this time.   For two years he used every available means to imbue his people with his own ideal for a church located as was this one in the midst of the masses.   He did not meet even with such response as was given him for several years in

Louisville. The congrégation and officers would support
him in every effort towards their own edification and the
extension of the work along accustomed lines, but they
had no desire for aggressive evangelization of the unchurched masses, nor did they welcome attempts to turn
the church itself into a home for all comers.

Dr. Simpson was always guarded in his references to
the attitude of this church, whose affection he greatly
prized, but on one occasion he related an illuminating incident. On the outbound trip of a church picnic, dancing
was commenced on the deck. When the pastor expostu-
lated, a church officer remarked that the young people
must have the worth of their money. A prolonged discussion was ended with the ultimatum that unless the
picnic were conducted in a becoming manner, the pastor
would state the facts on Sunday morning and appeal to
the congregation. Dancing was stopped forthwith. On
arrival at the park the pastor was wanted in every direction, until about four o'clock he slipped away, utterly
weary, to find a quiet spot for a few minutes' rest. He
had not gone far till he was attracted by music, and, his
suspicions aroused, he hastened in the direction indicated.
To his astonishment and chagrin he found that while
he had been kept busy with all sorts of demands, the young
people had been enjoying to the full the license granted
them by the church officials. It came to him as forceful
evidence that their ideals and his were irreconcilable and
was, as he confessed, one of the indications that his hopes
could not be realized.

In one of his last public utterances Dr. Simpson gave
by special request a number of reminiscences, one of
which referred to this crisis.

"For two years I spent a happy ministry with this

noble people, but found after a thorough and honest trial
that it would be difficult for them to adjust themselves
to the radical and aggressive measures to which God was
leading me. What they wanted was a conventional parish
for respectable Christians. What their young pastor
wanted was a multitude of publicans and sinners. Therefore, after two years of most congenial and cordial fellowship with these dear people, and without a strain of any
kind, I frankly told them that God was calling me to a
different work, and I asked them and the Presbytery of
New York to release me for the purpose of preaching the
Gospel to the masses."

This step was taken after much deliberation and a
week spent in his study in prayer. After discussing his
decision with the church session he announced it to the
congregation at a midweek meeting. His address was
from the text "The Spirit of the Lord is upon me, because
he hath anointed me to preach the gospel to the poor,"
and stated very simply and clearly his reasons for resign-
ing and his ideals for a work in this great city. A daily
paper reported that "as Mr. Simpson concluded, many
of his hearers sat with bowed heads and with handker-
chiefs at their eyes. Officers of the Thirteenth Street
Church corroborated Mr. Simpson's statement about good
feeling in every respect."

One of the issues which he faced at this time was the
administration of the ordinance of baptism. He had become convinced that the scriptural method was the baptism of believers by immersion and shortly before had
submitted himself to this rite. In presenting his resignation he made reference to this. "He had said to the
session what he need not have said, but he did not wish
to keep back even a minor matter, which he regarded as

infinitely subordinate to the great work of the Gospel, that he felt he had no right under the New Testament to administer baptism to any one who is not old enough to make a confession of faith in Christ. As a minister of the Gospel he had stood in this spot two years before, taking the installation vows that he believed and would teach all the doctrines of the church, and it would be false and dishonest for him, since he had changed his views, to remain. He had no intention of agitating this question. If he were a private member of the church, he could still remain and hold his views on Christian baptism, since he did not regard this as such a necessary ordinance that it would separate him from the communion of any evangelical church."

Dr. Simpson never entered into controversy concerning this ordinance, and only one of the more than one thousand of his published discourses is on this theme. In the Gospel Tabernacle, baptism was administered only to believers and by immersion, but no one was excluded from membership whose conscience was satisfied with infant baptism. His presentation of the identification of the believer with our Lord Jesus Christ in His death and resurrection was so clear that almost everyone who accepted this teaching sooner or later came to see that baptism in water is a recognition of this participation. Consequently many applied for baptism at the conventions who had no thought of leaving their church affiliations.

He made no plea for a following from among his flock, but advised them publicly and privately to remain in the Thirteenth Street Church. Consequently there was no division in the congregation, and not more than two members withdrew from fellowship. He never became a separatist. In conversation with an elder of the Presbyterian Church in Canada not long before his life work ended, he said, "Stay in the old church and give your testimony there. You are a blessing to my old friend, your pastor, and he and the church need you. Unless it becomes a matter of conscience, a choice between obedience to man and God, your place is where you are."

Nor did he try to deflect Christian workers from their associations, though he sorely needed help in those early days. Rev. Kenneth Mackenzie says: "As often as I could I met with him, for he seemed to long for me, and I was always blessed in fellowship with him. I confess I was more than once allured to think of following his step. In later years he once declared in public that he would much prefer to have Mr. Mackenzie's presence and teaching as a minister of the Episcopal Church than as a worker in the Alliance."

In due course Dr. Simpson's resignation was accepted by the congregation and the presbytery, his farewell sermon being preached on November 7, 1881. He had surrendered a lucrative salary of $5,000, a position as a leading pastor in the greatest American city, and all claim upon his denomination for assistance in a yet untried work. He was in a great city with no following, no organization, no financial resources, with a large family dependent upon him, and with his most intimate ministerial friends and former associates predicting failure. Dr. John Hall said to him, in presbytery: "We will not say goodbye to you, Simpson; you will soon be back with us."

Only seven persons were present at his first meeting which was held in November, 1881, in Caledonian Hall, Eighth Avenue and Thirteenth Street. One of this number was Josephus Pulis, the reformed drunkard, of whom

Mr. Simpson afterward said that he was once the greatest sinner but now the sweetest saint in New York City. From this first meeting until his death in 1914 Mr. Pulis was closely associated with the work.

In one of his choicest books, *The King's Business,* Dr. Simpson referred to that humble beginning. "I remember well the cold and desolate afternoon years ago, when a little band of humble, praying Christians met in an upper room to begin this work for God, and we opened our Bibles, and these words were just before us: 'Who hath despised the day of small things?' 'Not by might, nor by power, but by my spirit, saith the Lord of hosts.' We knelt before Him there and thanked Him that we were poor, that we were few, that we were weak, and threw ourselves upon the might of the Holy Ghost, and He has never failed us."

Three services were held on Sunday and two every day during the week, the afternoon gathering being for the training of workers. The evening service was preceded by street preaching and usually closed with an inquiry meeting where many souls were saved. It soon became necessary to secure a larger place, and Abbey's Park Theatre was taken for the Sunday evenings. A feature of these meetings was the singing of a large choir which filled the stage.

The next step, a still further venture of faith, is recorded in *In Heavenly Places:*

"Ten years ago when the Lord called me to step out into this work of faith and evangelization, He laid it upon my heart so strongly that I could not question nor resist that I was to take the Academy of Music. It seemed a very audacious and almost reckless thing to do in the feebleness and poverty of that young work, for few of us had any means and it would seem that these should be husbanded and economized to the utmost.

"But there was no doubt left of the Lord's mind, and I obeyed and committed myself to the work. Afterwards I could see God's wise and holy purpose in giving breadth and height to the span of the work which was in His mind and which He wished us to begin; and as we stepped forward, the way was opened, the means were provided at the last minute, and the work was inaugurated with a sweep of blessing which in no other way it could have received."

In this great auditorium a series of evangelistic services was held in which Dr. George F. Pentecost participated, and Mr. and Mrs. George C. Stebbins assisted in the service of song. Dr. Pentecost was one of the first prominent leaders to associate himself with these campaigns. His attitude is expressed in a letter sent to the editors when he heard of the passing of his friend, whom he was so soon to join in the presence of the Lord.

"With thousands of others I have heard with profound sorrow of the departure of Dr. Simpson to be with the Lord whom he loved and whom he so valiantly and faithfully served. I have known Dr. Simpson for many years, in fact, from before the time he came to New York from Louisville. A most lovable and courageous man, loyal to his deepest convictions, he launched out into the deep, cast his net on the other side of church, conventionalities, and took a great draught of fishes. His missionary zeal was astonishing and put to shame some of our older and more conservative boards. I have met some of his missionaries in various parts of the pagan world, and they all seemed animated by his spirit."

After this campaign they met in Steinway Hall, Fourteenth Street and Fourth Avenue, for the remainder of the winter. In May, 1882, Grand Opera Hall, Twenty-third Street and Eighth Avenue, was rented and was the center of the work for about two years. A tent was presented by Mr. Heller, a Newark merchant, and a site on Twenty-third Street, offered without solicitation by William Noble. An aggressive evangelistic campaign was conducted in this tent during the summer of 1882. The following summer, the tent work was located on Thirtieth Street near Seventh Avenue, in a section then the very heart of metropolitan sin and crime. A reporter wrote of the tent meetings, "Scores have been brought to conversion during the summer, and scarcely a less number have been completely cured of diseases, many being complaints of long standing that have baffled the best medical skill. A list of names of those who had been healed was given, and a number of these were visited, all of whom gave their testimony and evinced the most implicit belief in their healing."

The next place of meeting was unusual. On the second anniversary of Mr. Simpson's retirement from his city pulpit Madison Square Garden was transformed into some semblance of a chapel for the opening of a series of gospel meetings. It was seven years since the Garden had been devoted to religious services, the last occasion being when Messrs. Moody and Sankey drew large crowds to the revival meetings. After the special meetings the work returned to Grand Opera Hall.

In the spring of 1884, a more suitable home, known as the Twenty-third Street Tabernacle, was secured. At the opening service Mr. Simpson said: "I am reminded of a providence I dare not fail to speak of. We desired to secure this building, then an old armory, but a strong financial company, led by Salmi Morse, who had set his heart upon presenting the blasphemous 'Passion Play,' had secured it for fifteen years. We did not stop praying. One lady prayed 'O Lord Jesus, make the carpenters fit up that place for us. Make the Passion people just decorate and furnish it for us. We cannot afford to pay fifteen thousand dollars to do it ourselves.' God did put His hand on it, and He did stop the public production of that play. After spending seventy thousand dollars in remodelling the building, the project broke down, and the company gave up the lease. They offered to sell us their improvements for five thousand dollars. We prayed over it, and God stopped us from going too fast. The building was finally put in the market, and sold at auction, and the gentleman bought whom we prayed would buy it. The result is that we have been enabled to come in here without paying a penny for improvements."

Mr. Simpson left for England in 1885, and shortly afterwards, Mr. Henry Varley, one of the most gifted and effective of English evangelists, came unexpectedly in touch with the work in the Twenty-third Street Tabernacle, the outcome being that for six weeks in the heat of summer he conducted a most successful campaign. This provision was one of many providences discernible in the story of those early days. God's hand was so evident that nothing in the way of divine interposition excited surprise. In his subsequent visits to America, Mr. Varley never failed to appear on this platform, and was one of the most welcome speakers in the Tabernacle and the Alliance conventions.

CHAPTER 10

MANIFOLD MINISTRIES

THE first decade of Dr. Simpson's ministry in the new movement, of which quite unintentionally he became the leader, was an era of evangelism. Dwight L. Moody was at the zenith of his success. Major J. H. Cole and Major D. W. Whittle were holding campaigns in the power of the Spirit. L. W. Munhall, George F. Pentecost, and George F. Needham were at the beginning of their successful careers as evangelists. E. Payson Hammond was in the midst of a unique work for the conversion of children. J. Wilbur Chapman, R. A. Torrey, and the generation of evangelists, among whom they were preeminent, were being prepared to follow in the train of this greatest group of soul winners of modern times. Dr. Simpson himself had been profoundly influenced by Whittle, Moody, and Cole, and had become a recognized leader of a type of pastoral evangelism which changed the complexion of the ministry of hundreds of godly men. The true evangelist has had no warmer friend nor any wiser or more sympathetic counselor. He could overlook almost any idiosyncrasy if only he were assured that the man was truly a winner of souls. "Yes, but he is one of the Lord's children," he would say when criticised for his leniency.

His preaching never lost the evangelistic note though in his later years he could not answer the many calls for meetings in every part of the world. When insuperable burdens finally overwhelmed him, he was planning to resume his old-time every night meetings in the Gospel Tabernacle. He never attempted any work that had not for its object the salvation of souls, and all of his institutions at home and abroad have been a light brigade in the great movement for world evangelization.

It was to this that he attributed the blessing which attended his ministry. In the introduction to his little volume, *Present Truth,* he says: "Perhaps one reason why He has been pleased to bless the work which many of us are permitted so imperfectly to represent is because in some measure we may have caught His meaning and may be working out His plan."

The work around which all of the activities connected with Dr. Simpson's ministry centered was the Gospel Tabernacle. It was the outcome of his early evangelistic meetings in New York City.

In *Word, Work, and World,* which he began to publish in 1882, he says: "At first there was no formal organization, but as Christians began to unite in the work and converts to need a church home, it became manifest that God was calling the brethren thus associated to organize a Christian church for this special work according to the principles and example of His Word. After much earnest prayer on the part of the little flock, a meeting was held at the residence of the pastor on the tenth of February, 1882, and a church formally organized in the name of the Lord Jesus Christ consisting of thirty-five persons. In one year the actual membership of the church has grown to 217, and the stated Sunday evening congregations are 700. No assessments or pew rents are allowed, nor any unscriptural ways of sustaining the Lord's work."

Mr. Simpson was not following a wholly unbeaten

track in his church ideal. "My plan and idea of a church," he said, "are those which are exemplified in the great London churches of Newman Hall and of Spurgeon, comprising thousands of members of no particular class, but of the rich and poor side by side." He did not aim primarily, as many have supposed, at rescue mission work, for he wrote: "From the first it was not designed as a mission to the lowest and vicious classes, but as a self-supporting work among the middle classes, who have no church home." This was undertaken, as stated in the Manual and Constitution, "in a spirit of loving consideration for all our sister churches and a desire to work in the most courteous and harmonious relations with all evangelical Christians and congregations of every name."

As the Gospel Tabernacle was an independent church, it was necessary that it should have its own constitution, principles, and by-laws. These were exceedingly simple, the constitution consisting of only eight brief articles of less than five hundred words, yet covering the essentials of faith. Profession of living faith in the Lord Jesus Christ and the evidence of a consistent Christian character and life were held as the only conditions of membership, and baptism by immersion upon profession of faith was practised, but was not compulsory. The specific mission of the congregation was stated to be the evangelization of neglected classes both at home and abroad.

The atmosphere of the church was wholesome, and although it suffered much misrepresentation and caricature, the testimonies of sane religious leaders, which might be quoted at great length, prove that there was nothing extreme or fanatical either in the testimony or methods. In *The Christian Inquirer* of May 24, 1888, was the following sentence: "It is a mistake to suppose that Mr.

Simpson's work is mainly in the line of propagating the doctrine of divine healing, that being a subordinate feature. His chief work is purely evangelistic, and in many of the meetings physical healing is not referred to, but Christ as the sinner's Friend is the great theme." Speaking at the October convention in the Tabernacle in 1891, Dr. Ellinwood, Secretary of the Board of Foreign Missions of the Presbyterian Church, said, "I cannot but pray that God may speed you in your foreign missionary and every other part of your work in seeking to lead men from the power of Satan unto God. I rejoice in all you are doing."

The migrations of the congregation during the first five years have already been followed. From Twenty-third Street Tabernacle they removed in May, 1886, to The Church of the Disciples, an immense building at the corner of Madison Avenue and Forty-fifth Street, erected as a popular church center, where Dr. Hepworth and Dr. John Newman (afterwards Bishop Newman) had ministered. This was offered to them at about half of its value, and after much prayer was purchased.

The location proved to be less suitable than had been anticipated, and after two years an urgent demand for the property was accepted. For a few months meetings were held in Wendell Hall and Healey's Hall, while the Tabernacle at 692 Eighth Avenue was being erected. The plans included a book-store on the Eighth Avenue frontage with rooms for the Missionary Training College above it; Berachah Home, a six story building fronting on Forty-fourth Street; and the Gospel Tabernacle at the rear with corridors opening on both streets. The cornerstone was laid January 14, and the Tabernacle was opened on June 23, 1889. Thus, after occupying twelve places of worship in eight years, the congregation found a permanent home.

The Gospel Tabernacle was the center of the ever-increasing ministry which radiated from the life of Dr. Simpson until he rested from his labors. Here unnumbered thousands have been saved, sanctified, healed, and inspired by the blessed hope of the near coming of the Lord. It still continues to be the most aggressive center of evangelism in New York City. The poor are always welcome, and not infrequently drunkards stagger in through the corridor and go out saved by the grace of God.

A church with such various activities, with a congregation so widely scattered, and with such a standard of pulpit ministry as Dr. Simpson maintained required associate pastors of rare endowments. The energies of the senior pastor were more and more divided. Rev. A. E. Funk, who became assistant pastor in 1886, always had many duties in the Institute and in the Alliance. Several men of marked ability and spiritual power have been associated in the pastorate of the Tabernacle.

From 1891 till his death in 1908 Rev. Henry Wilson, D.D., was the greatly beloved associate pastor. He had been deposed from a curacy in Kingston, Ontario, by the bishop of the Church of England in Canada because he had gone to the altar in the Salvation Army barracks, but had been welcomed by Dr. Rainsford as senior assistant pastor in St. George's Protestant Episcopal Church in 1883. After coming to New York he had been marvelously healed and quickened in the Twenty-third Street Tabernacle. With Dr. Rainsford's approval, he had participated in the Tabernacle ministries; and when he accepted the associate pastorate in the Gospel Tabernacle,

Bishop Potter said his standing would be unimpaired. Consequently he maintained a communion service after the Episcopal order in the chapel of the Gospel Tabernacle regularly when in the city. He was Dr. Simpson's closest friend and most trusted fellow-worker, and his genial presence and spontaneous joy made him an untold blessing to the flock and the wider constituency all over the continent.

Rev. Milton Bales, D.D., a Methodist Episcopal minister, succeeded Dr. Wilson as associate pastor. Later, Pastor F. E. Marsh, from Sunderland, England, filled this office, lectured regularly in the Missionary Institute, and traveled widely in convention work. Rev. W. T. MacArthur, one of the first field workers of the Alliance, devoted his unique gifts to the Tabernacle during 1912 and 1913. Since that time Rev. Elmer B. Fitch, a product of the Tabernacle itself, has been assistant pastor.

Besides these regular pastors, many men with a message were heard in the Tabernacle pulpit. In the early days Dr. John Cookman, of Bedford Street Methodist Episcopal Church, was heart and soul with Mr. Simpson both in his city work and in convention tours. He was a gifted preacher and a man of rare spirituality, and his early death was an irreparable loss. Another Methodist minister, who from the first was associated with Mr. Simpson, was Rev. Henry C. McBride. The three made an admirable team for convention work. Someone, when asked about a meeting they conducted, said, "Simpson laid the fuel, Cookman kindled the fire, and McBride went up in the flames."

Rev. F. L. Chapell, D.D., who in his later years was principal of Gordon Bible College, Boston, a preacher of the prophetic type, was often in the Tabernacle pulpit, and Dr. Frederick W. Farr, for several years dean of the Missionary Training College, was one of the most frequent and acceptable substitutes in the pastor's absence. That prince of preachers, Dr. A. T. Pierson, was always warmly welcomed. In the more recent years the younger generation of Alliance leaders was frequently heard in this mother church. To its pulpit still come the most earnest preachers of the day, and not a few of the great leaders feel as does Dr. C. I. Scofield who, in his opening remarks at a convention, said that he considered it a high honor to be upon this platform, and indeed would have been disappointed if his friend, Dr. Simpson, had not invited him to be one of the speakers.

A German branch of the Tabernacle was begun in 1887 through the ministry of Rev. A. E. Funk and others, which has been used to spread the testimony among many of the German speaking residents of the city and which has added many of the most devoted and godly members to the congregation. Regular services in German have been conducted by Pastor Funk.

"From the first," wrote Dr. Simpson, "the highest aim of the Tabernacle has been to labor and pray to carry out the Great Commission. With this in view, *The Missionary Union for the Evangelization of the World* was organized in 1883." How fully this aim has been realized is proof of the clear vision which he received at the very beginning of God's plan and purpose through his instrumentality. John Condit and four others were sent to the Congo in November, 1884, the intention being to establish a self-supporting mission, but this first missionary venture failed of permanency. All of the later missionary efforts were conducted through the Society formed at Old Orchard in 1887.

Another phase of the missionary effort was the founding of the *Missionary Training College* in October, 1883. This opens such a large chapter in Dr. Simpson's life that Dean Turnbull will discuss it in a special contribution.

Though the movement was not a rescue mission, special efforts were made from the very beginning to reach the submerged element in the city, and such missions in New York and elsewhere look to the Alliance for the warmest sympathy and support. The closing day of the New York convention has always been devoted entirely to meetings for rescue missions, and draws together a large number of their leaders.

In 1885 two such missions were commenced. One of these, at Thirteenth Street, near Greenwich Street, was conducted and sustained entirely by the young men of the Twenty-third Street Tabernacle. The treasurer was Franklin L. Groff, who still continues in active association with the Tabernacle, and whose business genius has been used in his office as Financial Secretary of The Christian and Missionary Alliance to establish a thoroughgoing system in the work of the Society.

The other, known as *Berachah Mission,* instituted and conducted by Mr. and Mrs. Henry Naylor, was opened on Twenty-ninth Street near Ninth Avenue in the autumn of 1885. Mrs. Naylor had been wonderfully healed, and their life and fortune were consecrated to the Lord's service. They purchased a site at Tenth Avenue and West Thirty-second Street, and erected the best equipped mission in the city at a cost of more than thirty thousand dollars. It was dedicated on Mr. Naylor's fiftieth birthday, June 21, 1887, and for many years reached thousands of the most degraded and neglected of the people in this district which was then such a den of iniquity that it was known as Hell's Kitchen. It also maintained a special work for sailors. Dr. Dowkonnt, of the Medical Mission, held a free dispensary and gave medical attendance without charge to the poor of the neighborhood. Rev. Robert Henck was pastor and superintendent for some years, and after Mr. Naylor's death was united in marriage with Mrs. Naylor.

In 1889 a branch known as the *Eleventh Avenue Mission,* was opened on Eleventh Avenue near Thirty-eighth Street by converts and workers of the Berachah Mission where fruitful soul saving work was carried on.

As one of the earliest developments a service was opened in 1882 at 120 West Twenty-seventh Street for the salvation of the fallen women who crowded that part of the city. Mrs. Henry Naylor was the chairman of a committee of ladies who had this work in charge. This ministry has been continued under other auspices as the Margaret Strachan Home.

Mrs. E. M. Whittemore, like Mrs. Naylor, had received a great spiritual quickening when she was healed, and also devoted herself to rescue work for girls. In 1891 *The Door of Hope* was opened, and this mission has been one of the monuments to faith in God. It has always had the hearty co-operation of Dr. Simpson and the Gospel Tabernacle.

The South Street Mission also originated with the ladies of the Tabernacle but was taken up and wholly sustained by Mrs. D. W. Bishop, a friend of the work. It has been known for many years as *the Catherine Street Mission,* is under the superintendency of Miss Margaret Delaney, and is still in cordial fellowship with the Tabernacle.

The Colby Mission, Greenpoint, Brooklyn, was carried on and supported for twenty years by Mr. Charles Colby and his family, who had been inspired to service through Dr. Simpson's ministry. Rev. A. E. Funk assisted very frequently, especially in dispensing the ordinances.

The Eighth Avenue Mission was opened in 1899 by Miss May Agnew, the organization secretary, of the C. and M. A. and one of Dr. Simpson's most devoted helpers. Miss Sarah Wray, of England, joined her soon afterwards as her associate, and since Miss Agnew's marriage to Rev. H. L. Stephens has been the superintendent of this soul-saving station which is now located at 290 Eighth Avenue. There is no mission on the continent where the fullness of Christ is held forth to sinners with greater power and attractiveness, and perhaps no other that participates so actively in the work of foreign missions.

Various ministries for children were undertaken quite apart from the regular Sunday school work in the Tabernacle and missions. *Berachah Orphanage* was opened in the summer of 1886 at 329 East Fiftieth Street in answer to the prayers and under the oversight of Mrs. O. S. Schultz, who afterwards became joint superintendent with Mr. Schultz. After occupying various buildings in New York the Orphanage was located at College Point, L. I., the property being purchased through a gift by Mr. Joseph Battin. It also was a work of faith, and like all such had many testings. The first came almost immediately, when unsympathetic state officials closed it because it had not received a charter. But at the hearing the opposing party inadvertently read a clause of the law which gave the commissioners the privilege of granting a temporary license, and that very day the children returned to the orphanage..

The *Junior Missionary Alliance,* with a department known as the King's Lilies, was organized in 1891, with that lover of children, Dr. Henry Wilson, as president. Mrs. A. B. Simpson, the treasurer, and Miss E. M. Brickensteen, the secretary, devoted themselves to this ministry. A unique series of studies for children on the fourfold Gospel and missions was prepared and widely circulated. The children's meetings at the great summer conventions are still a feature of never failing interest, the contributions of the children being a revelation to many a wealthy church member who has been present at their jug breaking.

A number of young people's meetings and societies grew up, among which were the *Young Ladies' Christian Alliance,* commenced in a small prayer meeting at the first convention at Old Orchard, in 1886; the *Young Ladies' Christian League,* organized in 1891, of which Mrs. C. deP. Field was the leader; and the *Young Men's Crusade.* During recent years the *Young People's Alliance* has been a very vigorous and spiritual work, maintained in the Tabernacle by the younger members. Besides their own regular meetings they carry on meetings on the street, on shipboard, and work in the hospital. *The Young People's Association* in the Alliance branches is everywhere characterized by intense missionary zeal.

It would seem that no one life could support so many activities. Yet we have scarcely mentioned Dr. Simpson's literary and publication work, the Missionary Institute, Berachah Home and the ministry of healing, the great conventions with their distinctive features, nor yet the greatest product of his life, The Christian and Missionary Alliance. These are so distinct and important that a chapter will be devoted to each of them.

Into few lives has as much been crowded as the Spirit of God wrought in and through A. B. Simpson in the first decade of this larger ministry. Looking back over it, his own heart was hushed and solemnized, and he expressed something of what it meant to himself in these verses:

> "And what has the decade brought
>   For God, and man, and thee?
> O Master, sure it can mean to none
>   All it has meant to me.
>   O blessed years,
>   Begun with fears,
>   But spanned tonight
>   With rainbow light
>   For all eternity.
>
> "It has brought the richest work of life,
>   It has brought His healing power;
> It has given the dearest friends of earth
>   And countless blessings more.
>   O dear Decade,
>   Thy light and shade
>   Have seemed to fall
>   With Christ in all
>   **A joyful memory.**"

CHAPTER 11

CONVENTIONS AND TOURS

THERE has been no more unique feature in Dr. Simpson's ministry than the conventions which he and his associates have conducted in many parts of the world. They have been unlike all other gatherings, although partaking of many of the essential features of the usual camp meetings, conferences, and conventions. For one of the elements of Dr. Simpson's genius was his ability to adapt other men's methods to the specific aims and objects which he wished to attain. The fervor of the old time camp ground, the sweet fellowship of the Keswick meetings, the strong message of the best Bible conferences, the inspiration of prophetic gatherings, the aggressive note of evangelistic campaigns, and the world vision of missionary convocations—all mingled in these conventions. Saints and sinners, old men and young children, great spiritual leaders and babes in Christ—all found their portion of meat at this table. These gatherings were neither dull nor sensational, neither formal nor without order, neither without spiritual freedom nor given over to demonstrative extravagances. They were a puzzle to the professor of religious psychology and an enigma to the reporter, but to the hungry-hearted they were a feast, to the weary a refreshing, to the sick a fountain of healing, to the Christian worker an inspiration, and to the worn missionary a haven of rest.

The convention was the expression of Dr. Simpson's very life and personality. His simplicity, his humility, his graciousness, his freedom, his brotherliness, his deep insight into truth, his conservatism, his breadth of vision, his passion, and his supreme devotion to Christ seemed to pervade the very atmosphere and to control every meeting. He created a type that reproduced itself so that in the hundreds of conventions which he could not attend, the same spirit was manifest, and continues since his homegoing, in these great gatherings.

These conventions have done more than any other single agency, except Dr. Simpson's pen, to disseminate the truth which he so loved and to call men to the service in which his own life burned out. Sometimes critics were won by the atmosphere and the spirit which he manifested in a meeting where his masterful appeal was not heard. A lady who had consistently opposed her husband was induced to attend a Canadian convention. Dr. Simpson was announced as the principal speaker at the afternoon meeting, but his train was late, and the session was nearly over when he arrived. He slipped quietly in at the side door and with bowed head took a seat at the rear of the platform, quite unnoticed by the chairman. The gentleman nudged his wife and said, "That's him." She watched him for a moment, and then her eyes fell. She had expected to see some assertive demagogue, and the first glance revealed to her a man with the spirit of the Man of Galilee. He had won a friend and disciple. A Presbyterian minister from the south who was at Old Orchard, received a letter warning him against the theology of the Alliance. "Bless you," he wrote in reply, "their theology is all gone up in doxology."

These conventions began in the Twenty-third Street Tabernacle in 1884. The object was "to gather Christians of common faith and spirit for fellowship; to study the Word of God; to promote a deeper spiritual life among Christians; to seek a better understanding of the teachings of the Scriptures respecting our physical life in Christ; to wait upon the Lord for a special baptism of the Holy Spirit for life and service; to encourage each other's hearts in the prospect of the glorious appearing of the Lord; and to promote the work of evangelization at home and missions abroad."

At the second annual convention in the Twenty-third Street Tabernacle the speakers included Mrs. Baxter, of Bethshan, London; and Mrs. Stroud-Smith, from the Isle of Man; Dr. W. S. Rainsford and Dr. Henry Wilson, of St. George's Protestant Episcopal Church, New York; Dr. John E. Cookman, of the Bedford Street M. E. Church, New York; Rev. Kenneth Mackenzie, Jr., of the Church of the Holy Trinity, New York; Dr. T. C. Easton, East Orange, N. J.; Rev. H. W. Brown, Chicago; Miss Carrie F. Judd, now Mrs. George H. Montgomery, Buffalo; Rev. Charles H. Gibbud; Rev. Jacob Freshman, of the Jewish Mission; Josephus Pulis; Captain Lewis W. Pennington and Evangelist John Currie of Brooklyn; and Henry J. Pierson, of Boston.

This second convention in New York so impressed Christian workers that invitations came to hold similar meetings in the largest cities on the continent. The first series included Brooklyn, Buffalo, and Philadelphia in October, and Pittsburgh, Chicago, and Detroit in November and December, 1885. Some of these were held in large halls and others in leading city churches of various denominations. In spite of some adverse criticism, these meetings commended themselves to a wide circle in the Church. Rev. Dr. Spencer, pastor of the First Methodist Church, Chicago, where the convention was held, wrote indignantly concerning a telegraphic report of those meetings. "I have been very greatly pained to see an extract from the *Detroit Tribune* in reference to the convention held here by yourself, Dr. Cookman, and others. It is a scandalous libel and slander against you and your associates. I am not a believer in the particular doctrine of healing which you teach and did not sympathize with the anointing service, yet I want the more to be fair and candid. While many were not friendly to the convention, they could not but respect the decorum, the propriety, the solemnity of the services and especially the anointing service."

The *Herald and Presbyter* of Cincinnati, the leading Presbyterian journal of the middle West, contained the following account of the Pittsburgh meetings. "The Faith Cure Convention which was held in Pittsburgh drew both through curiosity and sympathy a goodly number, and excited much comment especially among Christian believers. There was no question of the sincerity and integrity of character of the more prominent leaders, and the testimony of those who declare themselves to have been healed was listened to with great interest and respect. This is not the place to enter upon a discussion of the merits of this special phase of belief, but it was pleasant to find the conference so entirely evangelical and so full of Christ. It had little of the characteristics which are ordinarily found in meetings of this kind; and, except for the ceremony of anointing with oil, was scarcely unusual in any way. This ceremony naturally excites curiosity, yet it was merely an evident attempt to fulfil the literal counsel of James."

In the same kindly spirit the *Michigan Christian Advocate* referred to the meetings in the Woodward Avenue

Congregational Church, Detroit. "This convention was to us personally a feast as rare as it was refreshing. All our aversion and prejudice, and we were full enough of both, disappeared under the genial and irresistible warmth of their ardent faith and what seemed to us their daring trust in God. Cranks they may be in the popular definition, but it is for the lack of just such crankiness that the Christian Church languishes today. If conversion to such a doctrine involves the masterly grasp of spiritual truth and that sublime nearness to God in prayer which characterizes these people, we cannot accept it too soon or too strongly. We were glad of at least one convention in which the methods of pastors and the failings of the Church were not held up for caustic criticism and biting ridicule and in which there was a genial recognition that we were one in the work of the Master. . . . There was noticeably an entire discrediting of self. The anointing was nothing; their agency was nothing; Christ was everything. It is not a small thing to have their faith and realizing sense of God's immediate presence with them, and this, they claim, was an integral part of their healing. They have their health, their spiritual elevation, and their keen enjoyment of unceasing labor for God. On the other hand, we have our invincible theories, our conventional piety, our unimpeachable orthodoxy, and our doctors' bills. Ought we not to be satisfied?"

The two great central conventions have been held annually in New York and Old Orchard Beach, Maine, where in 1881 Mr. Simpson met one of the great crises of his life during Dr. Cullis' convention. Half a mile from the shore there is a grove with a natural amphitheater. A number of annual religious conventions were held on this ground. Rev. H. Chase, one of the Camp-ground directors, attended the second convention in the Twenty-third Street Tabernacle, and there gave this testimony: "I have learned here to receive Christ in His fulness as never before, and I shall go home praising Him for a finished redemption, to live out His life in me and serve Him with all my heart. I cordially invite you all to Old Orchard next summer for a similar convention." Later an earnest request came from the directors of the Old Orchard Camp-ground for a conference for Christian Life, Work, and Divine Healing to be held for ten days in the summer of 1886.

The first Old Orchard convention was the outcome of these invitations and was held August 3-10, 1886. Among the speakers beside Mr. and Mrs. Simpson were Mr. W. E. Blackstone, Chicago; Dr. H. L. Hastings, of Boston; Dr. Henry C. McBride, Ocean Grove; George B. Peck, M. D., Boston; Mrs. Henry Pierson, Boston; Rev. John Cookman, D.D., Rev. Dr. Munger, Rev. A. E. Funk, Rev. C. N. Kinney, Mrs. Henry Naylor, Mrs. M. J. Clark, Mrs. O. S. Schultz, Miss Sarah Lindenberger, and Miss Harriet Waterbury.

The subject of missions was pressed upon this convention. Mr. Blackstone delivered an epoch-marking address on Tibet, the last great stronghold remaining to be captured for Christ. Such a profound impression was made that steps were taken to organize a missionary society to carry the gospel to Tibet and other unevangelized regions. It was this moving of God's Spirit at the first Old Orchard convention which resulted in the world-girdling missionary movement of which Dr. Simpson has been the leader. At the second convention the movement took definite form in the organization of what was then called *The Evangelical Missionary Alliance.*

The early days of August have ever since witnessed one of the most remarkable religious gatherings of modern times. Dr. Simpson himself always gave his best in a series of addresses, and for thirty-two years his Old Orchard missionary sermons were among the greatest missionary appeals ever delivered. He gathered around him on this platform and at the New York convention the most deeply spiritual leaders and missionaries of the world, among whom were Dr. Andrew Murray, Dr. Baedeker, Mr. Henry Varley, Dr. Harry Guinness, Dr. F. B. Meyer, Dr. J. Hudson Taylor, Pastor Stockmeyer, Dr. John Robertson, Rev. John McNeill, Rev. Barclay Buxton, Rev. Charles Inwood, Pastor F. E. Marsh, Rev. D. H. Moore, Rev. Charles Inglis, Pastor Joseph Kemp, and many others from abroad were heard from time to time. The list of Americans would fill pages. We may mention Dr. A. J. Gordon, Dr. A. T. Pierson, Dr. H. L. Hastings, Dr. R. A. Torrey, Dr. George F. Pentecost, Mr. D. L. Moody, Major D. W. Whittle, Major J. H. Cole, Dr. James A. Brookes, Dr. Ellinwood, Mr. W. E. Blackstone, Dr. C. I. Scofield, Dr. Nathaniel West, Dr. F. L. Chapell, Dr. James M. Gray, Dr. Charles A. Blanchard, Dr. J. Wilbur Chapman, Dr. Robert Stuart MacArthur, Rev. Henri De Vries, Dr. Robert Cameron, Dr. D. M. Stearns, Dr. Robert E. Speer, Dr. J. Campbell White, Dr. A. C. Dixon, Dr. W. B. Riley, Dr. Egerton Young, Dr. H. C. Morrison, Rev. Henry Frost, Rev. Seth Rees, Dr. John Oerter, Colonel Clark, Dr. Henry C. Mabie, Mr. Charles G. Trumbull, Colonel Henry Hadley, Mr. Sam Hadley, Mrs. Phoebe Palmer, Mrs. Margaret Bottome, and Miss Frances E. Willard. This does not include any of the great men who were an integral part of the Alliance.

Frequently the attendance at the New York convention overflowed the Gospel Tabernacle, and the services had to be held in some large neighboring theatre or in Carnegie Hall.

One of the proofs of the power of these great conventions was the attention given to them in the daily press. Sometimes a whole page was devoted in the New York and Boston papers to these reports. Cuts caricaturing Dr. Simpson and the audience and burlesque reports of the proceedings frequently appeared. Occasionally, however, a keenly incisive sketch was published. Sometimes it came from a wholly unexpected source. A reporter from the *New York Journal* called one day on Mr. Simpson and asked him, "Do you know when the Lord is coming?" "Yes," replied Mr. Simpson, "and I will tell you if you will promise to print just what I say, references and all." The reporter's notebook was out in a moment. "Then put this down: 'This gospel of the kingdom shall be preached in all the world for a witness unto all nations; and then shall the end come' (Mat. 24:14). Have you written the reference?" "Yes, what more?" "Nothing more." The reporter laid down his pencil and said, "Do you mean to say that you believe that when the Gospel has been preached to all nations Jesus will return?" "Just that," said Dr. Simpson. "Then," replied the reporter, "I think I begin to see daylight." "What do you think you see?" "Why, I see the motive and the motive-power in this movement." "Then," said Dr. Simpson, "you see more than some of the doctors of divinity." And the next morning the *Journal* constituency were given this simple dialogue with a most appreciative and sympathetic sketch of Dr. Simpson and his work.

The conventions in other cities have been one of the great outlets for the testimony of the Alliance. Unnumbered multitudes have heard the message who otherwise would never have been touched by it. Most of these have remained in their churches, themselves quickened into new life and their lives empowered for hitherto unthought of service. The ministry of many a pastor has been transformed. Hundreds have been called into Christian service who had never dreamed of such a life. A brilliant young woman, who was a court stenographer in St. Louis, was asked to report a convention in that city. Thinking it was a medical conference, she consented. She was amazed when Mr. Simpson rose at the beginning of the first meeting and said, "Let us pray." She was unconverted, but the Holy Spirit turned her heart to search after eternal realities, and before the year ended she had accepted Christ. She started to read the Bible, but "could not make head or tail out of it," so she went to the Moody Bible Institute. She is now known the world around as Miss Grace Saxe, Bible teacher of the Torrey-Alexander campaigns, and later of the Billy Sunday party.

When Mr. Simpson made his first trip to Great Britain during his Hamilton pastorate, he went as a tourist. When he returned in June, 1885, he was the most prominent delegate among hundreds from various lands at the Bethshan Conference. This conference brought together representative teachers on the Deeper Life from all parts of the world, some of the principal speakers being Dr. Simpson, Pastors Schrenk and Stocker, of Switzerland, and Dr. W. E. Boardman, Robert McKilliam, M. D., Mrs. M. Baxter, and Mrs. Katherine Brodie, of London. It began in Bethshan Hall, the headquarters of the work of

Dr. and Mrs. Boardman, but, owing to the large attendance, Agricultural Hall was secured.

In Liverpool large audiences assembled in Hope Hall where at one of the meetings more than eighty persons were anointed for healing. Other conventions were held in Brighton, Worthing, Blackheath, Newcastle and Edinburgh.

The last of the series was held in the beautiful Scottish capital. Writing of this meeting Mr. Simpson said: "When we were last in Edinburgh fifteen years ago, we were received with cordial kindness and hospitality by the Presbyterian friends in the great Assembly in May, and had the privilege of meeting many of the great and good men of that church, and even speaking in the Free Church Assembly Hall, in behalf of the Presbyterian Church in Canada. But now we were to represent a much less popular interest. Indeed, we were to stand under the suspicion of doubtful, if not false teaching."

Many ministers and medical students were in the audiences. At the first meeting a medical student tried to force a discussion on divine healing, though the subject had not yet been mentioned. The medical students connected with the Edinburgh Medical Mission were deeply impressed during the meetings and asked for a private conference, which the main body of medical students attempted to break up, but the wisdom given to Dr. Simpson, Dr. McKilliam, and the other leaders, prevailed. The series of conferences made a deep and lasting impression in Great Britain, and much fruit resulted in after days.

The most important journey abroad in Dr. Simpson's ministry was his tour of the mission fields in 1893. He left New York in January for Great Britain where he held important conferences with missionary secretaries, including Dr. Hudson Taylor and the leaders of the Church Missionary Society, addressed a number of large gatherings, and renewed precious fellowships with English friends.

A direct journey across the continent and the Mediterranean, a brief visit in Cairo and other Egyptian towns, a landing through the breakers at Jaffa, and he stood among sacred scenes. His brief visit to the Holy Land was one of the sweetest memories of his life.

> "Sweet Olivet, sweet Bethany,
> My heart shall oft remember thee"

is a couplet from one of several beautiful hymns and poems which he composed during that visit. He was kindly received by the missionaries of other societies in Jerusalem and assisted in the opening services of the Mildmay Mission Hospital at Hebron, then under the charge of Mrs. Bowie, of England. The Alliance had no mission in Palestine at that time, but Miss Lucy Dunn and Miss E. J. Robertson had been in Jerusalem for three years supported by friends of the Alliance. On Mr. Simpson's return to New York the Board decided to take up work in the land of our Lord.

The latter part of February and all of March were spent in India, visiting and encouraging the Alliance missions in the province of Berar, under the leadership of Rev. and Mrs. M. B. Fuller, and in a rapid survey of the work of other societies in the great cities of India.

As Rangoon and Singapore were ports of call, Dr. Simpson was permitted to touch the mission work in Burma and the Malay Peninsula. In Hong Kong, then the great missionary center for South China; Canton, the southern mercantile capital, and Macao, where Robert

Morrison landed as the first missionary to China, he made a careful study of the South China field where a little company of Alliance missionaries were preparing for the great pioneer work which was to follow. Similar studies in Central China, where the Alliance had established a mission, and in the north, where Miss Duow and others were located in Peking, occupied the remainder of his two months' visit to this great empire. He had not time to enter Manchuria where the Swedish Alliance Mission had been started in the previous year.

Dr. Simpson's three weeks' journey through Japan was arranged by Dr. and Mrs. T. Gulick of Kyoto, the ancient capital, who afterward took the oversight of the Alliance work then in its inception in this island empire. On July 7 he left Yokohama and, after a call in the mid-Pacific at Honolulu, reached San Francisco and crossed the continent, arriving home just in time for the Old Orchard Convention.

In all the countries visited Dr. Simpson was warmly welcomed by other missions. He addressed numerous regular gatherings as well as specially arranged meetings and conferences, and gave in spiritual blessing quite as much as he gained in knowledge of the mission field.

A full account of this deputational tour was published in *Larger Outlooks on Missionary Lands,* a volume which is replete with information about the lands which had been visited.

One paragraph, written in Japan, touches his family history. "From across the great seas came also the message that our own dear mother had just gone to join our revered and honored father in the home above. We thanked our Heavenly Father for her fourscore years and the sweet memory of her life and love, and for our dear and venerable father, who, at eighty-four, had just a little while ago passed on before. How much of the rich blessing that has crowded our life is due to their faithful prayers! Thank God for their precious lives and everlasting memorial."

In January, 1910, Dr. Simpson left New York for another missionary journey. He called at St. Thomas in the West Indies, at several Brazilian cities, spent a week in our Argentine missions, sailed around Cape Horn, visited Chile and the Alliance missions in that republic, touched Peru, then Ecuador, where a few Alliance missionaries are almost alone as light-bearers of the Gospel, and thence journeyed homeward by way of Panama. There he was exposed to a contagious fever which, but for answered prayer, would have subjected him to detention in the pest house. He felt that it had been permitted to enable him to enter more fully into the testings which the missionaries endured in tropical climates. This trip so greatly enlarged his missionary vision that he said he had discovered South America.

In the Spring of 1911 Dr. Simpson again visited Great Britain, his last tour abroad. He was accompanied by Dr. R. H. Glover who had just arrived from China on furlough, and Pastor F. E. Marsh, of Bristol, England, who had arranged a series of conventions extending over a period of nearly three months, and covering nearly all the principal cities from London to Dundee. Dr. Simpson also preached in many of the large churches and was welcomed by such Christian leaders as Dr. F. B. Meyer, Dr. R. F. Horton, Rev. Samuel H. Wilkinson, Rev. Joseph Kemp, Rev. W. Graham Scroggie, Rev. J. Barclay Buxton, Rev. D. H. Moore, Rev. Cecil Polhill-Turner, and Mr. Louis P. Nott. Besides this series of conventions, the party was invited to participate in several of the well known stated conventions for the deepening of the spiritual life.

This deputational visit added thousands to the friends which Dr. Simpson had already made in Great Britain. Nowhere was his message and ministry more greatly appreciated, and he received pressing invitations to return for service in an even wider sphere, but this was one of the many calls to which he was never able to respond. The reverence so manifest in British audiences and the sincerity evidenced in both criticism and approbation found a responsive chord in Dr. Simpson's heart, and he highly prized the fellowship of the large circle who knew him face to face and the greater number to whom his writings were as the words of a father in Israel.

CHAPTER 12

THE MISSIONARY VISION

I T is evident that Albert B. Simpson, like Paul, the apostle to the Gentiles, had been separated from his birth unto a missionary ministry. His mother had dedicated him to this high calling. When he was a few weeks old, he was baptized by the Rev. John Geddie, who was on the eve of departure to Aneityum, in the South Sea Islands, as the first Canadian missionary, and who consecrated the child to missionary service. In sending out this pioneer, the Presbytery of Prince Edward Island laid the foundations of the great foreign missionary work of the Presbyterian Church in Canada. And what a foundation! The epitaph on Geddie's tomb on the island of Aneityum reads: "When he landed in 1848, there were no Christians; when he left in 1872, there were no heathens." In the passion of that consecration prayer this missionary apostle begat a son in his own likeness.

The prayer made an indelible impression on John Geddie's memory. When on furlough twenty-one years afterward, he sought out James Simpson and inquired for the boy whom he had dedicated. On being informed that he was preaching in Hamilton, licensed but not yet ordained, Mr. Geddie immediately visited the young minister and informed him that in his baptism he had been devoted to the proclamation of the Gospel.

Another great missionary hero deeply affected his life. His sister says, "When Albert was about nine years of

age, he read the life of Rev. John Williams, the martyr
missionary of Erromanga, and was so impressed with it
that he devoted himself to the work of the Lord, and he
never swerved from his determination."

It may have been John Geddie who aroused the parents to a world vision of the Church's work, but whatever
the cause, the Simpson home had a missionary atmosphere.
If the mother consecrated the babe to telling out the
story, the father did not fail to lead the family to the
throne of grace for their friend in Aneityum and his fellows on the outposts of service, for he had a deep interest in missions. One of Mr. Simpson's classmates, who
was stationed in the Presbytery of Chatham, testifies
that James Simpson, the representative elder of his congregation, was one of the missionary forces in the presbytery.

The call of a waiting world which had come to the
lad, was not lost in college; and when Albert Simpson
graduated, he still desired to offer himself to the Church
for its foreign service. These claims and the calls from
important home centers were weighed, and, after consul-
tation with his betrothed, the invitation to Knox Church,
Hamilton, was accepted. A marked increase in missionary interest was noted in that congregation during his
ministry.

It was while pastor in Louisville that the crisis came
which turned the whole course of A. B. Simpson's life.
Part of that upheaval affected his relation to foreign
missions. He had gone to the Believers' Conference at
Watkins Glen in 1878, for rest, refreshing, and physical
recuperation. Mingled with the teaching of the deep
things of God, for which his heart was hungering, there
was a strong missionary note for which his mind and

spirit had been undergoing a long course of preparation. He left the conference deeply stirred, and went west to visit friends near Chicago for further rest and waiting on God. There the burden of a Christless world was rolled upon him by the Spirit of God. In a sermon preached in August, 1894, on *The Macedonian Cry,* he tells how the *vision* came to him.

"Never shall I forget how, eighteen years ago, I was awakened one night from sleep, trembling with a strange and solemn sense of God's overshadowing power, and on my soul was burning the remembrance of a strange dream through which I had that moment come. It seemed to me that I was sitting in a vast auditorium, and millions of people were there sitting around me. All the Christians in the world seemed to be there, and on the platform was a great multitude of faces and forms. They seemed to be mostly Chinese. They were not speaking, but in mute anguish were wringing their hands, and their faces wore an expression that I can never forget. I had not been thinking or speaking of the Chinese or the heathen world, but as I awoke with that vision on my mind, I did tremble with the Holy Spirit, and I threw myself on my knees, and every fibre of my being answered, 'Yes, Lord, I will go.'

"I tried for months to find an open door, but the way was closed. Years afterward God showed me that He had laid the question on my heart, and until He allowed me to go forth, if I ever did, I was to labor for the world and the perishing heathen just the same as if I were permitted to go among them."

When Mr. Simpson decided to turn his back on the inviting prospect of an ever-widening ministry at home and "depart far hence unto the Gentiles," he immediately wrote to Mrs. Simpson, telling her of his decision, and asking her to unite with him in this new consecration and to be ready to go with their children to China as soon as the way opened. The missionary vision had not yet come to Mrs. Simpson. She had been willing to leave her loved Canada at the call of the people of the sunny south. But China! Her practical nature, her mother instinct, and perhaps her womanly ambition for her brilliant husband all answered *No*. Looking back on it all now, she herself tells the story. "I was not then ready for such a sacrifice. I wrote to him that it was all right —he might go to China himself—I would remain at home and support and care for the children. I knew that would settle him for a while."

He did not lose his vision. Not for others, but as his heart's deepest expression he wrote,

> "To the regions beyond I must go,
>   Where the story has never been told;
>   To the millions that never have heard of **His love**,
>   I must tell the sweet story of old."

Yet in the light of what has come to pass, no one can now believe that the Spirit of God had planned a place for him in China. The Lord of the Harvest had larger designs, a mightier ministry for this man whose life He had been moulding from his birth. First of all, however, his heart must go to the ends of the earth to be chained there in endless bondage to the cry of the unevangelized millions of heathen lands, of the Moslem world, aye, and of the scattered sons of Israel. Hence his enthralled heart was ever singing his own plaintive song:

> "A hundred thousand souls a day
>   Are passing one by one away,

In Christless guilt and gloom.
  Without one ray of hope or light,
With future dark as endless night,
  They're passing to their doom."

Mrs. Simpson is our authority for saying that it was this cry from heathen lands, rather than the call of the metropolis with its unevangelized multitudes, that decided him to accept a pulpit in New York. He wanted to be at the center, in touch with the lines radiating to the ends of the earth. Moreover he had a well matured plan for an illustrated missionary monthly, and with that unerring instinct which so often led him to the right trail, he knew that such an enterprise should be launched in New York.

It was a daring proposal. He was laughed at alike by publishers and missionary leaders. They did not know that a new force had appeared, who, like every leader, was a decade or two ahead of his times. He pursued his purpose, and though he broke physically and mentally under the strain, *The Gospel in All Lands* was established, and in other hands remained for years the pioneer and pattern of illustrated missionary periodicals.

There was a charm about his presentation of the missionary claim that appealed alike to young and old. He was so in love with his Master's plan for the redemption of the world that he never failed to make it appear fascinating and arresting. Dr. Harlan P. Beach, Professor of Missions in Yale University, said: "Do not forget to mention as one of his great achievements the institution of a pictorial review. Dr. Simpson was the first to make the missionary story beautiful and attractive." No keener judgment was ever passed upon his ministry.

The great battle cry of the Student Volunteer Movement has been *The Evangelization of the World in This Generation.* John R. Mott said truly, "No other generation but ours can evangelize the present generation," and years ago Robert E. Speer boldly defended the evident premillennial viewpoint of the watchword. Both of these aspects, *responsibility* and *immediacy,* were marked in Dr. Simpson's conception of our relation to missions. In one of his too little read books, *The Christ of the Forty Days,* he states this with his usual incisiveness. "It is a very simple and a very awful *responsibility,* and looking in the face of every one of us, the Master simply asks, 'Are you going to do what I tell you, or not?' There is no possibility of evasion. He simply says, 'Go ye,' and we must go or disobey." And again—"Unless I am sure I am doing more at home to send the Gospel abroad than I can do abroad, I am bound to go; and if He wants me, I am ready to go whenever He calls and makes it plain. This and this alone is the attitude of fidelity on the part of each of us to this sacred word of our departing Lord."

To him the *immediacy* of the need arose, not merely from our responsibility to the men of our own generation, but, even more, from the plan of God for the working out of the salvation of all mankind. He believed that God is visiting the nations, "to take out of them a people for his name," and that,

"After these things I will return,
And I will build again the tabernacle of David, which is fallen;
That the residue of men may seek after the Lord,
And all the Gentiles, upon whom my name is called,
Saith the Lord, who maketh these things known from of old."
(Acts 15:16-18.)

This links missions inseparably with the second coming of our Lord. It was this point of approach that made Dr. Simpson's teaching of the second coming so wholesome and practical, and missionary work a service of love to our coming King.

His great missionary text was Matthew 24:14, "And this gospel of the kingdom shall be preached in all the world for a witness unto all nations; and then shall the end come." He firmly believed that this is the business of the Church during this dispensation and a necessary preparation for the coming of the Lord. In an early number of *Word, Work and World,* he wrote: "The last great missionary movement therefore will be a universal proclamation of the Gospel of the Kingdom. Is this the ordinary gospel message? Or is it a special proclamation of the advent and the reign of Jesus? Young translates it, 'this Gospel of the reign.' It is the midnight cry, 'Behold, the bridegroom cometh; go ye out to meet him.' Already it is beginning to sound over Christian nations. But it is a cry which the heathen must hear, and which will awake the slumbering nations as no other call."

This affected his ideal for the Church. He expressed it forcefully in a paragraph already quoted from his address at the opening of the new church edifice in Louisville. His heart was gladdened as he saw his ideal becoming a reality in the Gospel Tabernacle. That work was born with a missionary passion. When it was a year old, it formed a missionary society, and, in its second year, it sent five of its members to the Congo. When it moved to the Madison Avenue Tabernacle, the pastor was able to say in his opening sermon, "I am glad this church has some members today in India, though it is a little church of only four or five years' growth. I am glad it has some members in Central Africa today, some in England, and some in almost every state in the Union. Oh, I trust the day will come when we shall count them by thousands in foreign lands. I believe the greatest purpose of God in sending us here, next to preparation for His coming, is to send the Gospel everywhere."

No leader ever saw his ideal embodied in a movement more perfectly than Dr. Simpson's missionary passion has been reproduced in his followers. The Alliance branches may sometimes have neglected to provide adequately for their superintendents, but they have never failed when the missionary offering was called for. The leaders themselves may be straitened, but no personal need ever prevents an Alliance worker from pressing the missionary appeal. The pledges received at the local annual conventions are even more of a marvel to the public which observes them than the first great offerings were at Old Orchard and New York City. The only explanation that can be offered is that which Dr. Simpson gave to a reporter of the *Syracuse Herald:* "Put this down," he said; "our people love to give." "Yes," said the reporter, "I have it. What more?" "That is all," replied Dr. Simpson. And when the reporter witnessed the manner in which the offering was made, he had to admit that, strangely enough, the people seemed to love it.

It was no desire to lead a movement that induced Dr. Simpson to organize The Christian and Missionary Alliance. Here is his own statement of the principles which should guide in such an undertaking. "No new society should be organized to do what is already being done by some other society. If there is some new principle to be worked out, some new method to be proved, some new agency to be employed, or some wholly unoccupied region to be reached, it is all right to attempt it, provided the movement is wisely planned and carried out by experienced and consecrated men. But simply to repeat what is being done somewhere else, or to start a new society because Hudson Taylor, Dr. Guinness, Andrew Murray, or somebody else has started a society, will simply prove like the echo of the parrot's voice as it tries to repeat the empty sound that has fallen upon its ear."

The foregoing is the negative, but here is a positive word with reference to *The Evangelical Missionary Alliance,* as the society organized was first named. "The Evangelical Missionary Alliance has been formed as a humble and united effort on the part of consecrated Christians, in all parts of the land and world, to send the Gospel in its simplicity and fullness, by the most spiritual and consecrated instrumentalities, and the most economical, practical, and effectual methods, to the most needy, neglected, and open fields of the heathen world."

There was no "at home and abroad" in Dr. Simpson's conception of missions. When he lifted up his eyes on the fields, they were everywhere white unto the harvest. To him the multitudes of New York and our great American continent were as sheep without a shepherd, just as were the vaster multitudes in the deeper darkness of heathen lands. He was never happier or more effective than when doing the work of an evangelist, and in the last year of his life, when unequal to public ministry, he would be found at the altar tenderly winning and mightily interceding for souls. The missionary conventions under his direction always gave a large place to evangelism. His ideal for the Missionary Institute was that it should be a training school for effective witnesses in our own land and in the regions beyond. He expected the same spirit of sacrifice from those who remained at home, whether in definitely appointed Christian work or as witnesses at their daily tasks, as is manifested in our missionaries, and the crowning glory of his leadership was that this ideal was attained. The whole Alliance echoes his song,

"We all are debtors to our race;
    We all are bound to one another;
The gifts and blessings of His grace
    Were given thee to give thy brother;
We owe to every child of sin
    One chance, at least, for hope of heaven;
Oh, by the love that brought us in,
    Let help and hope to them be given.

"No more noble monument to the beloved founder of The Christian and Missionary Alliance, and its leader through the more than thirty years of world-wide service, could possibly be erected than that already reared in heathen lands, bearing evidence to the fact that Dr. Simpson was true to God, true to the vision which God gave him of missionary work in many lands, and true to the message of the fullness of Christ which was to be proclaimed." In these words Rev. Alfred C. Snead, Assistant Foreign Secretary, expressed the thought in many minds as they reviewed the life of this man of God. Dr. Glover, with his graphic pen, will sketch this monument. One day we shall all see it. Faces brown and black, yellow and white, are being built into it—living stones, chosen and chiseled after the Master Builder's pattern. Some one of Dr. Simpson's spiritual children may find the last stone in some yet closed field, and then the King Himself will come.

CHAPTER 13

THE CHRISTIAN AND MISSIONARY ALLIANCE

MR. SIMPSON'S second trip to Great Britain was made in response to an invitation to take part in an international convention which had been called by Dr. W. E. Boardman, to meet at Bethshan, London, in June, 1885, at which delegates were present representing many of the forward movements and associations for the deepening of spiritual life in all parts of the world.

This gathering strengthened Mr. Simpson's conviction that the time was ripe for an association of believers in the fullness of the Gospel. An editorial in *Word, Work and World* in October of that year speaks of the need of "A Christian alliance of all those in all the world who hold in unison the faith of God and the gospel of full salvation."

In the year book of the Christian Alliance for 1893 Mr. Simpson stated the platform and purposes of this organization which later became The Christian and Missionary Alliance.

"The Christian Alliance was organized in the summer of 1887 at Old Orchard convention for the purpose of uniting in Christian fellowship and testimony in a purely fraternal alliance the large number of consecrated Christians in the various evangelical churches who believe in the Lord Jesus as Saviour, Sanctifier, Healer, and Coming Lord. It seemed to very many that there was a divine necessity for a special bond of fellowship among those who were being thus simultaneously called into closer intimacy with our coming Lord in order that we might give a more emphatic testimony to these great principles which might well be called at this time 'present truths,' that we might encourage and strengthen each others' hearts by mutual fellowship and prayer, and that we might unite in various forms of aggressive work to give wider proclamation to these truths and prepare for the coming of our Lord. With this view the Alliance was formed and founded upon the special basis of the Fourfold Gospel as above expressed. In all other respects and with reference to all other doctrines its attitude is strictly evangelical.

"It is not an ecclesiastical body in any sense, but simply a fraternal union of consecrated believers in connection with the various evangelical churches. It does not organize distinct churches or require its members to leave their present church connections. There is no antagonism whatever in the Alliance to any of the evangelical churches, but a desire to help them in every proper way and to promote the interest of Christ's kingdom in connection with every proper Christian organization and work. Its organization is extremely simple, consisting of a central executive Board in New York, incorporated under the laws of the state with auxiliaries and branches in the various centers of population."

Any Christian could become a member of the Christian Alliance by signing this simple creed: "I believe in God the Father, Son, and Holy Ghost, in the verbal inspiration of the Holy Scriptures as originally given, in the vicarious atonement of the Lord Jesus Christ, in the eternal salvation of all who believe in Him, and the everlasting punishment of all who reject Him. I believe in the Lord Jesus Christ as my Saviour, Sanctifier, Healer, and Coming Lord."

Where a group of members existed, they formed a local branch of the Alliance with stated monthly or weekly meetings and in some places a local superintendent. A number of such branches constituted a state auxiliary with regularly appointed officers, of whom the state superintendent was the active head. A group of states formed a district, under a district superintendent. The superintendents were voluntary or honorary workers, but, as the movement progressed, it became necessary for many of them to devote their entire time to this ministry. The faith principle was carried out, the central organization contributing nothing to the support of these workers, though in later years state and district superintendents have been granted a small allowance to assist them in the work.

Rev. E. J. Richards, Home Superintendent of the Society, gives this summary of the organized work: "At the present time there are between three and four hundred branches and connected churches in the United States and Canada. There are twenty officers known as secretaries or department heads, district superintendents and field evangelists, about two hundred located pastors and local superintendents, twenty-five evangelists devoting their whole time to revival campaigns, and fifty to seventy students of both sexes from the Bible schools, who are pouring out their lives in the neglected sections of the home field, winning souls for Jesus and getting splendid training for aggressive work in the regions beyond."

At the Old Orchard Convention in 1887 a missionary organization known as *The Evangelical Missionary Al-*

liance was also effected. The Principles and Constitution then adopted are so fundamental to The Christian and Missionary Alliance that a synopsis is given.

It will be undenominational and strictly evangelical.

It will contemplate the rapid evangelization of the most neglected sections of the foreign mission field.

It will use thoroughly consecrated and qualified laymen and Christian women as well as regularly educated ministers.

It will encourage the principles of rigid economy, giving no fixed salaries.

It will rely upon God to supply the necessary means through the freewill offerings of His people.

It will endeavor to educate Christians to systematic and generous giving for this greatest work of the Church of God.

It will form auxiliaries and bands in all parts of the country for the promotion and extension of its objects.

It will be governed by a board of directors elected annually, who shall appoint and direct the missionaries employed.

It will leave each church established on the foreign field free to organize and administer its affairs as it may choose, provided that such method be scriptural in its essential features.

In November, 1889, after conference with friends in Canada, this missionary society was incorporated as *The International Missionary Alliance.* Dr. Simpson was the General Secretary of the Board, and upon him fell most of the executive and administrative duties for several years. David Crear, a successful business man of New York City, was treasurer, and has ever since given his services freely in that office, devoting much of his time and a large portion of his income to the Alliance work.

The International Missionary Alliance was supported chiefly through the Christian Alliance, and the two societies were virtually one in purpose and in constituency. Consequently in 1897 they were united formally and legally under the name of *The Christian and Missionary Alliance*. Rev. A. B. Simpson was elected President and General Superintendent; Rev. A. E. Funk, Secretary; David Crear, Treasurer; and Mrs. A. B. Simpson, Financial Secretary. There was also a Board of Managers consisting of twenty-four members, including the above named officers. This amalgamation not only simplified the management but also brought the home and foreign fields into even a closer relationship, and The Christian and Missionary Alliance has been in a unique way a foreign missionary institution. Its local workers at home are never heard appealing for their personal support, but there are no more earnest advocates for foreign missions. The Alliance conventions have been, if possible, even more missionary in spirit than formerly, and the climax of every convention is the missionary offering.

The increasing demands on the administration and the necessity for fuller supervision of the home work resulted in a revision of the constitution at the Annual Council in May, 1912. Without interfering with the duties of the executive officers, departments were created, each with an executive secretary. These include the Finance Department; the Home Department, which has supervision over all of the work in America; the Foreign Department, which directs the different missions abroad; the Deputation Department, which has charge of missionary literature and deputations; the Publication Department, which is responsible for the preparation and issuing of books and periodicals; and the Educational Department, which has general supervision over the Training Institutes in the United States which are recognized by the Board. This system of administration has proven to be a great blessing to the work and relieved the pressure which was overwhelming the executive officers.

It is doubtless largely on account of this increased attention to details that the Society has had a perhaps unequalled record in the fearful years of testing during the great world war. Although allowances have been greatly increased owing to the higher cost of living, and the demands for transportation and expenses on the fields have been nearly doubled, it has been possible to appropriate full allowances every month since 1914 and to remit all necessary expenditures for station work. The native staff has been increased, new stations opened, buildings erected, and a score or more of missionary recruits added each year.

The principles upon which the Alliance is organized were the expression of Dr. Simpson's own convictions and attitude. From the outset he deprecated every tendency to separativeness from other Christians either in spirit or in organization. Yet he saw that unless great wisdom and much Christian forbearance were shown on the part of the Alliance leaders and teachers, a line of cleavage would almost imperceptibly appear, and the Society would tend in the direction of sectarianism. He used constant vigilance and much wise diplomacy to prevent any of his associates from departing from the vision which had been given of the work. With pen and with voice he frequently restated the stand originally taken. In the *Alliance Weekly* for November 11, 1899, he had this to say on the mission of the Alliance:

"Let us never forget the special calling of our Alliance work. It is not to form a new religious denomination. It is not to duplicate a work already done. It is not to advocate any special system of theology. It is not to glorify any man or men. It is first to hold up Jesus in His fullness, 'the same yesterday, and today, and forever.' Next, to lead God's hungry children to know their full inheritance of privilege and blessing for spirit, soul, and body. Next, to witness to the imminent coming of the Lord Jesus Christ as our millennial King. And finally, to encourage and incite the people of God to do the neglected work of our age and time among the unchurched classes at home and the perishing heathen abroad. God will bless us as we are true to this trust."

Again, we find him writing in the same organ in 1912: "While the Alliance movement to a certain extent is unavoidably a self-contained organization and requires a sufficient amount of executive machinery to hold it together and make it effective, yet we must never forget that it has a certain interdenominational message for the Christian Church today and that this ministry must not be clouded by any narrow sectarian tendencies that would alienate the sympathy of those in the churches that are open to our message. There are cases continually arising where it is necessary to provide special and permanent religious privileges for little bands of Christian disciples who have either been converted in some evangelistic movement or pushed out of their churches by false teaching and harsh pressure and prejudice. Yet these local and independent congregations should never be considered as Alliance churches in any technical sense, but simply independent movements which God Himself has specially raised up 'through the present distress' and over which we exercise for the time a certain spiritual oversight."

Dr. Simpson always maintained the distinction between an Alliance branch and an independent church. Replying in an issue of *The Alliance Weekly* of 1913 to a correspondent who asked whether it is consistent for Alliance branches to dispense ordinances, receive and dismiss church members, and perform other church functions, he said: "The acts and functions referred to are entirely proper on the part of an independent church which may be affiliated with the Alliance, but are not consistent in a regular Alliance branch. The same company of people may have a double organization. They may be on the one hand a church organized and properly legalized under an independent charter, and as such be in fellowship with the Alliance, but entirely controlling their own property and worship. At the same time many members of this congregation or church may be united in an Alliance branch which enjoys the hospitality of the church. This is the case with the Gospel Tabernacle, New York City, the oldest, perhaps, of these independent churches."

So, too, Dr. Simpson never swerved from his determination to hold the movement true to the great fundamentals of the Gospel, and to insist that healing and other phases of the testimony be kept in a properly subordinate place. In the report of the dedication of the Midway Tabernacle, St. Paul, the headquarters of the work of District Superintendent Rev. J. D. Williams, on Dr. Simpson's last deputational tour in December, 1917, this statement appears: "He took occasion to emphasize in the strongest possible way the fact that the primary objective of the Alliance movement was not the teaching of special doctrines, but the salvation of souls and the reaching of the neglected classes from whom the conventional methods of modern churches were steadily creating a distressing gulf of cleavage and separation. He trusted that this should always be the primary ideal and aim of our work."

A society with such principles could not hope to build up a great, visible organization. It was always a great satisfaction to Dr. Simpson to know that the message had reached and permeated multitudes who had no outward connection with the Alliance. He had no sympathy with any tendency to exclusiveness or with self-centred little gatherings of the saints, nor yet with the mere aim to build up a work. To him, an Alliance branch, however small, was a lighthouse in its own community and a recruiting station for the little army of good soldiers of Jesus Christ which had been sent to the ends of the earth.

Yet this motive and ideal was the strength of the organization. Factions might divide it and false fires might burn a local branch to ashes, but the Alliance would always emerge with new vigor, because two or three disciples with "Jesus in the midst" constituted a unit of this society.

The Alliance was regarded by the public as the personal work of a great leader. Thousands kept asking "What will become of the Alliance when Dr. Simpson is gone?" The answer was given in the last year of his life when he was not in active leadership. His absence from his pulpit, from the great conventions, and from the editorial chair and the executive offices was keenly felt, yet there was no falling off at any point, and the missionary offerings were larger than ever before. Since he was laid at rest, almost another year—the period of supreme test of his principles and methods—has passed, and the Society is in the midst of an advance movement all along the line. This is the surest testimony that can be given that he had received and obeyed a heavenly vision in the development of the movement known as The Christian and Missionary Alliance.

CHAPTER 14

THE MINISTRY OF HEALING

THE ministry of healing was never wholly lost from the Christian Church. The testimony of Irenaeus, Tertullian and others shows that it continued during the first three or four centuries. It was revived by the Waldenses in the Middle Ages. Martin Luther claimed that Melancthon had been miraculously healed. Remarkable instances of supernatural healing occurred in the ministry of George Fox and the early English Friends, and authentic cases are narrated in the lives of Peden, Cameron, and other Scottish Covenanters. George Whitfield was raised from what seemed to be a death-bed and that same night preached the Gospel. John Wesley declared that anointing was a Christian ordinance designed to be permanent in the Church. In the last century Dorothea Trudel and Pastors Zeller, Blumhardt, and Schrenk on the Continent, and Dr. W. E. Boardman in England were greatly used of God in the healing of the sick. In America, Dr. Charles Cullis, a physician of Boston, Ethan Allen, a venerable minister of Hartford, and others exercised this ministry with remarkable results.

In the Old Orchard covenant Dr. Simpson solemnly promised to use the blessing he had received for the glory of God and the good of others. Some time before, when studying the Scriptures with a brother minister, his friend said, "Yes, Simpson, I see that healing is part of our privilege, but then we cannot preach it." To which A. B. Simpson replied, "I do not yet clearly see that it is part of the Gospel for today; but if I ever do, I must preach it."

Rev. Kenneth Mackenzie, who was in close touch with Dr. Simpson from the beginning of this ministry, says: "Had he renounced divine healing he could have obtained a wider and more tolerant recognition. But that would have required a diplomacy of which he could never be guilty. He would be true to God as God had led him to see truth, come what might. And now we find that it was the healing element in his initial work that proved most influential. The Friday afternoon meeting became a shrine for thousands of people connected with the churches of the city and its suburbs. From that meeting radiated streams of blessing that sanctified homes and hearts and parishes."

Referring to the early days, in one of his last addresses, Dr. Simpson said, "Sanctification and divine healing were not crowded upon the popular audiences who were not prepared for such strong meat, but some of the week-day meetings were appointed for the purpose of teaching and testifying along these lines."

The Friday meeting, which began in Mr. Simpson's parlors, has been carried on uninterruptedly for thirty-eight years. It often crowded the auditorium of the Gospel Tabernacle and is still one of the most spiritual gatherings in the Alliance work. An address on divine healing, and testimonies from those who have been healed are given, and requests for prayer are received from all over the world. The meeting always closes with an anointing service, according to the instruction given in the epistle of James.

Dr. Simpson was always careful to direct those who were anointed to look to the Lord and not to the anointing or the anointer, and very frequently took a very subordinate part in such services lest the eyes of any one should be turned to himself. As early as 1883 we find him writing, "It is very solemn ground and can never be made a professional business or a public parade. Its mightiest victories will always be silent and out of sight, and its power will keep pace with our humility and holiness. We solemnly warn the people of God against caricatures and counterfeits of this solemn truth, which they may expect on every side. We greatly deprecate the indiscriminate anointing of all who come forward, of which we hear in various quarters. We trust no one will take this honor unto himself, but 'he that is called of God, as was Aaron.' We hope the wonder-seeking spirit will not be allowed to take the place of practical godliness and humble work for the salvation of men."

Among believers in divine healing, anointing with oil has been frequent in connection with prayer in private for the sick. Though the elders of the church, where such are available, are usually called upon, many others, both men and women, have anointed the sick in the name of the Lord, sometimes disregarding Dr. Simpson's warning.

Mr. Simpson soon felt impelled to open his home for personal ministry to the afflicted. The Lord had been preparing the way for this by a work of grace in Mrs. Simpson's heart and life. She had been very slow to believe that God was leading her husband out of the ordinary channels of life and service into the way of faith and sacrifice. The difference in point of view became acute when their little daughter was stricken with diphtheria. True to his faith, he determined to commit the case into the hands of the Great Physician. Mrs. Simpson bitterly opposed this course, and finally, late at night, left the child with him declaring that she would hold him responsible for the consequences. He lay down beside the little girl, took her in his arms, soothed her to sleep, and committed her then and forever to the keeping of the Lord. At daybreak, when Mrs. Simpson entered the room, she refused to accept the assurance that the child was better, but a careful examination showed that every trace of the disease had disappeared. Without a further word, she turned away, went to her own room, and, shutting herself in, cried to the Lord to reveal Himself to her. That was the turning point in her life, and shortly afterwards she consented to the proposition to open their home to God's suffering children.

On Wednesday, May 16, 1883, a company of Christian friends assembled in their home at 331 West 34th Street for its dedication as a Home for Faith and Physical Healing. The announcement stated that "any sufferer who is really willing to *exercise* and *act* faith for healing will be received for a limited time for instruction and waiting upon God for temporal and spiritual blessing."

The following paragraph of a recent personal letter from Miss Fanny A. Dyer, of Chicago, tells of her visit to this home in 1883. "I had never heard much of the doctrine of divine healing when I entered the Friday meeting. On Sunday morning while preparing for breakfast, without being able to give much more Scripture for it than the promise of James 5:14-16, I was instantly healed, as gloriously and supernaturally as was the centurion's son. A new era began in my life for spirit, soul, and body, glorious beyond expression."

In her life story, published in a periodical some years ago, Mrs. Katherine H. Brodie tells of her stubborn refusal to consider the testimony of her friends, Mrs. Margaret Bottome and others, concerning divine healing.

Finally she attended the Friday meeting and was invited
to the Home. "I longed," she writes, "to accept the invitation but had not the courage to leave the hospital
and my remedies, and I feared the opinions of my husband and my friends. Later I attended another of Mr.
Simpson's meetings and, in obedience to the command in
James 5:14-16, was anointed and solemnly dedicated to
the Lord. Then followed ten days in the Home on
Thirty-fourth Street where precious lessons were learned
and glorious work given me for my Master. All pain
left; the Lord had become my strength. I wrote my
husband of my new life, but he, failing to understand,
hastened to New York, fearing I had gone wrong. Nine
months afterwards he became convinced my healing was
not mere fancy, and seeing my isolation, he sent me to
New York again; and whereas before he had been opposed to Mr. Simpson's work, now he arranged that on
our arrival we should go to his new Berachah Home."
Mrs. Brodie has since had a most fruitful ministry in
Great Britain and has visited America several times, ministering in the power of the Holy Spirit in Berachah
Home and at the Alliance conventions.

One year after the Home was begun, Mr. E. G. Sel-
chow, who himself had been marvelously healed, do-
nated a building at 328 West Twenty-third Street. On
May 5, 1884, it was formally dedicated to the Lord
under the name of *Berachah Home*, meaning "The House
of Blessing." It was moved to a larger house on Sixty-
first Street and Park Avenue, and in March, 1890, to the
six story building at 258-260 West Forty-fourth Street,
adjoining the present Gospel Tabernacle. In 1897 Rev.
Ross Taylor's beautiful residence on the Nyack hillside
was purchased and enlarged. To this delightful spot

Berachah Home was removed where for twenty years hungry hearts and broken bodies found refreshing and healing.

When Berachah was opened on Twenty-third Street, it was put in charge of Miss Ellen A. Griffin and Miss Sarah A. Lindenberger. Miss Griffin, who had been an active worker in city missions, had been wonderfully healed and devoted her remarkable gifts, until her death in 1887, to ministering in most practical ways to the suffering ones in the Home. Miss Lindenberger, a member of a wealthy and worldly southern family, had been in Mr. Simpson's congregation in Louisville. She was led by the Spirit into the mysteries of grace and to the devotion of her culture and enduements to a life of ministry in Berachah Home, remaining in charge until, on account of age, she was unable to continue this exacting service and the Home was closed. It is now one of the dormitories of the Missionary Institute.

Dr. Simpson himself gave much time to Berachah Home, and nowhere was his graciousness, sympathy, and power in prayer more manifest. Dr. John Cookman, Dr. Henry Wilson, Rev. A. E. Funk, Rev. Stephen Merritt, Rev. F. W. Farr, Rev. W. T. MacArthur, Mrs. A. B. Simpson and her sister Mrs. E. J. McDonald, Mrs. Margaret Bottome, Mrs. C. deP. Field, Mrs. Bishop, Miss Harriet Waterbury, Miss Minnie T. Draper, Mrs. E. M. Whittemore, Miss Ella G. Warren, and Mrs. O. S. Schultz were among those much used of the Lord in this Home and in the Friday meetings. During the years it was located on Forty-fourth Street, the ministry of Josephus Pulis was blessed to thousands. Among the medical doctors who were in full sympathy and frequently took part in these ministrations were Dr. George B. Peck, and Dr. James B. Bell, of Boston, and Doctors Barnett, Stevenson, and Brown, of New York. Dr. Scudder of New York had an attack on divine healing ready for the press when he became convicted that he should investigate for himself. He did so, was convinced of the truth, and became a warm friend of the work.

A number of other Homes were directly or indirectly connected with Mr. Simpson's ministry. *Bethany Home,* Toronto, was maintained for many years through the faith of Mrs. Fletcher and the Rev. John Salmon. Homes of rest and healing have been conducted by Miss S. M. C. Musgrove, of Troy, N. Y., and Mrs. J. P. Kellogg, of Utica, N. Y., and Mrs. Dora Dudley, of Grand Rapids, Mich. *Kemuel House,* Philadelphia, was under the personal care of Mrs. S. G. Beck, assisted by Dr. and Mrs. Cliff. In later years *Hebron Home* has been the center of the activities of Rev. and Mrs. F. H. Senft, and the headquarters of the Alliance in that city. In 1894, Rev. E. D. Whiteside, a Methodist Episcopal minister, whose prejudices had been overcome by hearing Mr. Simpson in the Twenty-third Street Tabernacle, and who had been marvelously healed, established a Branch of the Alliance and a Home in Pittsburgh, Pa. That successful business man, William Henry Conley, a member of the Alliance Board, was closely associated with Mr. Whiteside in that work.

Dr. Simpson's ministry as a teacher of the New Testament revelation of physical healing was far-reaching. More than any or all of its exponents he formulated this truth and by positive emphasis separated it from current fallacies. Even the secular press was impressed by his clear-cut presentation. *The New York Sun* of September 16, 1888, contained a full page interview in which it stated that "The friends who are represented by A. B. Simpson never use the term 'faith healing' or 'faith cure.' They always say 'divine healing' because they believe that faith has no power to cure anybody intrinsically, but that the real power in every case of true healing must be a personal God and not a mere subjective state of mind in the person concerned or anybody else."

Dr. Simpson never was anointed for healing, and though he taught that ministers should pray for and anoint the sick, he emphasized the right of the believer to claim healing directly for himself. How simply he states that "the Lord Jesus has purchased and provided for His believing children physical strength, life, and healing as freely as the spiritual blessings of the Gospel. We do not need the intervention of any man or woman as our priest, for He is our Great High Priest, able to be touched with the feeling of our infirmities, and it is still as true as ever, 'As many as touched him were made whole'." Thousands, who had no circle of believing prayer surrounding them, were thus, encouraged to trust the Great Physician.

His philosophy of healing was not couched in metaphysical terms. What could be plainer than this statement: "There are three epochs in the revelation of Jesus Christ through divine healing. The first is when we see it in the Bible and believe it as a scriptural doctrine. The second is when we see it in the Blood and receive it as part of our redemption rights. But the third is when we see it in the risen life of Jesus Christ and take Him into vital union with all our being as the life of our life and the strength of our mortal frame." And again, "This, then, is the nature of divine healing. It is not the mere restoration of ordinary health, but it is the impartation of the strength of Christ through the Holy Ghost, and it is often most marked alongside of the greatest physical weakness."

In a general way all devout Christians accept the first position. The second, that healing is a provision of the atonement, has been and is still bitterly opposed, even by some who pray for the sick. The third, or mystical view of participation with the living Christ in His resurrection life, taught by John and Paul and restated by A. B. Simpson, has been even less understood. Yet this became normal life to him and is interwoven in all of his writings. In this imparted life many a missionary "in deaths oft" has triumphed. It was the secret of the paradox of Dr. George P. Pardington's later ministry, who, though for years had to be carried to and from his classes, never missed a lecture in the Missionary Institute. It made Henry Wilson's life radiant with buoyant, joyous health. It healed Rev. G. Verner Brown of spinal meningitis and sustained him in a strenuous ministry. It enabled "The little man from Chicago," as Rev. W. F. Meminger called himself, to rise from a consumptive's couch and startle audiences up and down the continent with his hallelujahs. It is the distinctive testimony of the Alliance as to healing.

Most of the caustic criticism by well-meaning friends would be turned into prayer for those who take this position if the following quotations from Dr. Simpson were properly understood. The first reveals the secret source of this life. "We do not possess this strength in ourselves; it is the strength of Another, and we just appropriate it, and so Christ is our life. It is not self-contained strength, but strength derived each moment from One above us, beyond us, and yet within us."

Quite as essential are its terms. "The conditions of this great blessing are first that we are wholly yielded to Him, so that we should use the life He gives for His glory and service. Second, that we believe without doubt the promise of His Word for our own physical healing. Third, that we abide in Him for our physical life and draw our strength moment by moment through personal dependence upon Him."

Both Dr. Gray and Mr. Mackenzie call attention to the sanity exhibited by A. B. Simpson in regard to the practical application of his theory of healing. He was no extremist, whatever follies or fanaticisms some of his followers may have fallen into. The great preservative was the central and dominant truth of his whole system— Christ in you. He expected nothing from you, nor yet from himself, and was disappointed only with manifest rejection of Christ. How tender he was to those who failed! How considerate of those who had not seen the truth that to him was all in all!

Nothing that could be written would exhibit this so clearly as a leading editorial elicited by letters asking "Why are they not healed?" Dr. Simpson replied:

"First of all," we would say, "we do not know, and probably you do not know and will not know absolutely, until 'we know even as we are known'; and one of the first lessons that God wants you to learn is to be still and dumb with silence, suppressing every thought, trusting where you cannot see, and judging 'nothing before the time, until the Lord come, who both will bring to light the hidden things of darkness, and will make manifest the counsels of the heart.'

"It is quite shocking how some people get upon the throne and sit in judgment on God's providences, dealing

His judgments upon the heads of their brethren, and explaining the mysteries of His will as though they were His special interpreters and vicegerents.

"One of His supreme thoughts in many of His dealings is to teach us to be still, and know that He is God. But, while this is true, there are many lessons which He would have us learn when we are ready to do it with intelligent and earnest faith, and it may be that some of these thoughts will be helpful to anxious, perplexed minds. Therefore, we would say:

"I. That undoubtedly some persons have not been healed because their lifework was completed, and their Lord was calling them to Himself. There comes such an hour in every accomplished life.

"II. Sometimes, however, this is not fully understood by the suffering one or the surrounding friends, and there is the natural struggle and the earnest prayer, and the deep disappointment when it seems unanswered. But we believe that if we shall wait upon the Lord in a life of faith, obedience and communion, the heart will usually be able, with quietness, to understand enough of His will to triumph even in death itself.

"III. Sometimes, we believe, life is shortened by disobedience to God. Long life is promised to those who obey Him and follow Him; and of others it is said: 'For this cause many are weak and sickly among you, and many sleep. For if we would judge ourselves, we should not be judged. But when we are judged, we are chastened of the Lord, that we should not be condemned with the world.' This, undoubtedly, has reference to physical judgments, and the way they may be escaped is by self judging and holy, watchful obedience.

"IV. There is often a lack of real faith on the part

of the sick even where the external conditions of faith have apparently been fulfilled, and others may suppose there has been real faith in God for healing.

"Faith for divine healing is not mere abstinence from remedies, an act of intellect or will, or a submission to the ordinance of anointing, but it is the real, spiritual touch of Christ, and it is much more rare than many suppose.

"There is plenty of faith in the doctrine, plenty of readiness to give up remedies, plenty of faith in the prayers of others—especially if they are eminent saints— plenty of faith for healing in the future; but personal, real faith that takes Christ *now*, and, pressing through the crowd, touches His garment, is not much oftener found now than in the days when only *one*, struggling through the crowd that surrounded Him, really touched Him."

CHAPTER 15

AUTHOR AND EDITOR

ONE of the psalmists was so taken up with the glories of the King that he sings,

> "My heart overfloweth with a goodly matter;
> My tongue is the pen of a ready writer."

No such spiritual impulsion moved Solomon when he said,

> "My son, be admonished:
> Of making many books there is no end;
> And much study is a weariness of the flesh."

In his early ministry A. B. Simpson knew the laboriousness of much study and yet seems to have followed Solomon's admonition as to the making of books, for though his sermons frequently appeared in current papers, he had not given the public the fruit of his studies in permanent form.

When he was filled with the Spirit, it became literally true that his tongue was the pen of a ready writer, for his messages flowed so fluently from his lips that a stenographic report needed little editing. His sermons appeared almost verbatim in his periodical, and afterwards in book form.

It was because of this unusual gift that the making of many books was not an endless "weariness of the flesh," but one of the supreme joys of his ministry. Unquestionably he had great natural endowments. In his first two pastorates he prepared his sermons with the utmost care, writing and rewriting them, thus acquiring skill in literary art. "I had a facile pen," he once said in speaking of his experiences when he launched out in a life of faith, "and thought to support my family by literary work. But the Lord checked me from commercializing my gift." While he consecrated his talents and culture, he came to realize their insufficiency for the work to which God had called him and applied the great secret which he had learned to this as to every other activity.

In that heart message at Bethshan he said with characteristic humility: "Then I had a poor sort of a mind, heavy and cumbrous, that did not think or work quickly. I wanted to write and speak for Christ and to have a ready memory, so as to have the little knowledge I had gained always under command. I went to Christ about it, and asked if He had anything for me in this way. He replied, 'Yes, my child, I am made unto you wisdom.' I was always making mistakes, which I regretted, and then thinking I would not make them again: but when He said that He would be my wisdom, that we may have the mind of Christ, that He would cast down imaginations and bring into captivity every thought to the obedience of Christ, that He could make the brain and head right, then I took Him for all that. And since then I have been kept free from this mental disability, and work has been rest. I used to write two sermons a week, and it took me three days to complete one. But now, in connection with my literary work, I have numberless pages of matter to write constantly besides the conduct of very many meetings a week, and all is delightfully easy to me. The Lord has helped me mentally, and I know He is the Saviour of our mind as well as our spirit."

To the same inner working of the Spirit of God Dr. Simpson attributed his ministry of song. Though his reminiscences show that he recognized the maternal influence in his poetic temperament, a letter written not long before he laid down his pen stated that he had never written a poem in his life until the Spirit of God filled him with "psalms and hymns and spiritual songs." So, too, he speaks of his love for music and of his early, unaided attempts to master the violin. He did not have a musical education, yet a few of his musical compositions which seemed to flow from his heart spontaneously with the hymns to which they are set, have already been recognized in church music. Both words and music of *Everlasting Arms; Search Me, O God; Thy Kingdom Come,* and others touch the heart chords so strongly and tenderly that they will live in our hymnody.

The Gospel in All Lands, which Mr. Simpson instituted during his pastorate in the Thirteenth Street Presbyterian Church, was the first illustrated missionary magazine on the American continent, and, with one exception, the first in the world. He received little encouragement when he proposed to issue this monthly. But he had caught the vision of a needy world and believed that no art was too good for missionary propaganda. The first volume which appeared in February, 1880, assured its success, and although he was compelled by the physical collapse which occurred in the following summer to turn the magazine over to others, he had set such an editorial standard that for many years it held a foremost place in current missionary literature.

In 1882, shortly after Mr. Simpson's independent work began, he issued the first number of another illustrated missionary monthly, *The Word, Work, and World.* Some of his best literary work was done on this magazine. He was laying the foundation for his comprehensive grasp of world wide missions and giving his constituency the fruit of his studies in illuminating articles and readable paragraphs. All of the freshness of a newly found message is in the sermons which appear in these volumes. Leading articles on phases of the deeper life were always included, and some of his courses of lectures in the Training College, rich in Biblical scholarship, appeared in outline.

In January, 1888, the name of this magazine was changed to *The Christian Alliance,* as a few months before, the society bearing that name had been organized, and Mr. Simpson desired to make the paper the mouthpiece of the work. It continued as a monthly for more than a year and then became *The Christian Alliance and Foreign Missionary Weekly.* For a number of years it has appeared under the simpler title of *The Alliance Weekly.*

In outlining the policy of the paper in its new form as *The Christian Alliance and Foreign Missionary Weekly,* August 4, 1889, the editor made this announcement:

"The great movement of today, the greatest movement of the Church's history is a *Christ movement;* a revealing in our day, with a definiteness never before so real, of the person of the living Christ as the center of our spiritual life, the source of our sanctification, the fountain of our physical life and healing, the Prince-Leader of our work, and the glorious coming King, already on His way to His millennial throne and sending on as the outriders of His host and the precursors of His coming the mighty forces and agencies which today are arousing the Church and convulsing the world.

"This is the chosen and delightful ministry of this humble journal and the blessed circle of disciples who gather around the standard of the Fourfold Gospel; not merely to preach salvation, or sanctification, or healing, or premillennialism, but Jesus Christ.

"Therefore over all other names and themes we write our eternal watchword 'Jesus Only,' and devote these pages to the person and glory, the control, service, and exaltation of the Lord Jesus Christ."

As its editor, Mr. Simpson became recognized as one of the strongest editorial writers of our time. From week to week he compressed his richest experiences and profoundest knowledge in a few expository paragraphs, and scarcely a number left the press without one or more incisive editorials on the great providential movements and the trend of the times. He was most careful of the choice of his writers, and perhaps no paper has ever been at once so rich in spiritual food and so free from the taint of fanaticism. The missionary columns were filled with the triumphs of the Gospel not only in the Alliance fields but in the work of other societies of a kindred spirit.

For several years beginning July, 1902, Dr. Simpson also edited a high class religious monthly known as *Living Truths,* his own contributions showing the maturity of his literary work, and the articles by Dr. Wilson, Dr. Farr, Dr. Pardington, and others being of permanent value.

Among those who assisted Dr. Simpson in the details of editorial work were Miss Harriet Waterbury, Miss Louise Shepard, Miss Emma F. Beere, and Dr. J. Hudson Ballard, their ability and devotion making his editorial ministry possible.

In the early days Mr. Simpson's Sunday morning sermon appeared in separate serial form as *Tabernacle Ser-*

mons and had a wide circulation. In 1889, when his periodical became a weekly, as the discourse appeared in the paper, *Tabernacle Sermons* was discontinued. The demand for them had been so great that it became necessary to issue them in more permanent form.

In 1886 a book of sermons on service appeared under the title *The King's Business,* and another series covering the deeper life as presented in the books of the New Testament was issued in the same year entitled *The Fulness of Jesus.* Among the other early books of sermons may be mentioned *The Christ of the Forty Days,* or the revelation of the risen Christ, a theme on which Mr. Simpson loved to dwell; *The Love Life of the Lord,* which places him with Robert Murray McCheyne and Hudson Taylor as an interpreter of the mystical Song of Solomon; *The Life of Prayer,* showing as deep penetration into this mystery as Andrew Murray's discussions; *The Larger Christian Life,* revealing the possibilities of a Christ-centered and Spirit-filled life; and *The Land of Promise,* presenting our inheritance in Christ as typified in the conquest of Canaan. Many of his later sermons were also grouped into books.

The first volumes of his unique commentary, *Christ in the Bible,* appeared in 1889. This series was intended to include a survey of the great truths of the Word as revealed book by book. The best of his expository discourses were adapted to this purpose.

Four little volumes covering the essentials of Dr. Simpson's message were among his earliest productions and have had an enormous sale, both in English and other languages. They are in reality textbooks of the Alliance movement. *The Fourfold Gospel* is a brief statement of the four aspects of the Alliance watchword, "Jesus Christ

—Saviour, Sanctifier, Healer, and Coming King"; and
the others: *The Christ Life, Wholly Sanctified* and *The
Gospel of Healing* treat of phases of this truth.

Dr. Simpson has written a number of other books on
the distinctive testimony of the Alliance. *The Discovery
of Divine Healing, Inquiries and Answers Concerning
Divine Healing, A Cloud of Witnesses,* and *Friday Meeting Talks* deal with divine healing. His earliest book on
the Lord's Coming was *The Gospel of the Kingdom. The
Coming One,* written in 1912, is a general discussion of
the second coming; and a companion volume, *Foregleams
of the Coming One,* a survey of the prophecies of our
Lord's return was left in manuscript form, for later publication. *Back to Patmos,* an interpretation of the book of
Revelation, his latest contribution on this subject, was
written at the beginning of the war. He did not adhere
either to the historic or the futurist view in his interpretation but took middle ground where an increasing number of devout interpreters stand.

He was not an extremist on typology, but his three
books on *Divine Emblems in the Pentateuch,* together
with *Christ in the Tabernacle, Emblems of the Holy Spirit*
and *Natural Emblems in the Spiritual Life* make clear
the meaning of most of the typical passages in the
Scriptures.

The two large volumes, *The Holy Spirit in the Old and
New Testaments,* contain the fullest and clearest general
survey on the person and ministry of the Holy Spirit that
can be found in religious literature.

Polemical discussion had no attraction for Dr. Simpson. He had a positive message and usually left heretics
and fanatical teaching alone. He loved to tell of the Mis-
sissippi pilot who justified his lack of knowledge of the

location of the snags in the river by saying, "I reckon I know where the snags ain't, and there is where I propose to do my sailing." One of his strongest books is *Present Truth,* a series of discussions of the supernatural, in which he puts all opponents of true Christianity on the defensive by his clear presentation of the great facts which transcend natural law. In another book, *The Old Faith and the New Gospels,* he gives a most masterly arraignment of those unchristian phases in education, theology, sociology, and experimental life which have been seeking to discredit and supplant the orthodox view of Christ.

The great missionary messages which so thrilled multitudes unfortunately have been left unarranged. His *Larger Outlooks on Missionary Lands,* in which in his racy style he surveyed the fields which he visited on his tour in 1893, is his only book on missions.

Among his most widely read books are several volumes prepared for private or family devotions. The most popular has been *Days of Heaven upon Earth* with a message for each day of the year.

Though there is not a phase of Christian life or experience that is not touched in these books, several others were devoted to special aspects of the deeper life, reiterating and enlarging the great central theme "Christ in you the hope of glory." He never allowed himself to be drawn away from this one great message.

During the last two years of his active ministry Dr. Simpson devoted much of his time to the Bible commentary, in which he was condensing his life study of the Bible in the form of a Bible correspondence course. He had just begun the third and final year of this study when his pen was laid down. It was his ardent hope that he would be permitted to complete this work, but this expectation was not realized.

Dr. Simpson's early hymns were included in the first volume of *Hymns of the Christian Life,* which was published in 1891. This was followed by two other volumes in which a number of his later hymns appeared. The three books were afterward rearranged and combined, making a volume which has had a very wide circulation, and has greatly enriched modern hymnology.

In 1894 a number of Dr. Simpson's earliest poems were issued in a little volume, *Millennial Chimes.* This was the only book of poems which he published. Some songs that are not in the hymnal appeared in his periodicals, and a number were sent out as Christmas and New Year's messages. He wrote class songs for many of the graduating classes in the Missionary Institute, some of which, like *Be True,* have become widely popular. *Larger Outlooks on Missionary Lands* contains several of his finest missionary poems. *Beautiful Japan* was written as he left these "Islands of the Morning." Our hearts thrill with his as we read—

> "Land of wondrous beauty, what a charm there lingers
>   Over every landscape, every flower and tree!
> But a brighter glory waits to break upon thee
>   Than thy cloud-capped Mountain or thy Inland Sea,
> 'Tis the Father's glory in the face of Jesus;
>   'Tis the blessed story of redeeming love.
> Wake to meet the dawning of the heavenly sunrise!
>   Rise to hail the glory shining from above!"

Some of his unpublished poems have been collected recently and, together with old favorites, issued under the title, *Songs of the Spirit.* Quite a number still remain in manuscript. Here are some stanzas of one, entitled *The Star of Bethlehem*—

Celestial star in orient sky,
  Pointing to where the Babe is dwelling,
Whence dost thou come from worlds on high?
  What is the message thou art telling?

I came from realms no eye can see,
  Where vaster worlds of light are burning;
My orbit sweeps immensity,
  And ages pass ere my returning.

I came because a Star has shone
  Unseen upon your night of weeping;
The Son of God has left His throne,
  The Light of Heaven is yonder sleeping.

He bids you shed His radiance first
  Like Bethlehem's Star on lands benighted;
His earliest beams on Magi burst,
  So darkest lands should first be lighted.

Some day I'll come to these old skies,
  O'er all my path once more returning.
Lift up your hearts, lift up your eyes,
  And let your lights be always burning.

Bright Star, thy coming must be near;
  The darkness of the night gives warning.
Behold the sky begins to clear!
  The night is almost gone—Good morning!

Dr. Simpson wrote more than seventy books, but by far the greatest was the imprinted volume of a Christ-centered and Spirit-filled life. Of the making of this book he was keenly conscious when he wrote in the concluding words in his Commentary on Romans, "Beloved, the pages are going up every day for the record of our life. We are setting the type ourselves by every moment's action. Hands unseen are stereotyping the plates, and soon the record will be registered and read before the audience of the universe and amid the issues of eternity."

CHAPTER 16

A MAN OF ACTION

ALBERT B. SIMPSON always lived a strenuous life. When he was fourteen, he was taking a man's place on a Canadian farm. His high school course was cut short by a serious breakdown from over-study. The pace he set for himself in both of his early pastorates resulted in enforced periods of rest which he could not be induced to complete. When at length he was renewed in mind and body by the impartation of divine life, he devoted his new-found energies to the service of his Lord with a consecration which has rarely been equalled. Believing implicitly that this supernatural life had no limit within the sphere of duty and opportunity, he never stopped to measure his strength against the task before him.

He was an ambitious man and might have attained greatness in more than one sphere in life, but after the great crisis all of his aspirations were concentrated into those three passions which overmastered him and led him to declare: "I am ambitious to be quiet; I am ambitious whether at home or absent to be well pleasing unto Him; I am ambitious to preach the gospel where Christ has not been named." Because A. B. Simpson attained the first mentioned ambition to a degree that few have known, and lived in the repose of God, he was able to sustain an activity that amazed his friends and silenced the charge that his teaching led to passivity.

Returning to his pulpit in Louisville after a long, enforced absence in 1879, he preached on the text "This one thing I do." The following paragraph from his discourse shows that in those dark days he had learned Paul's secret of service. "The last thing in Paul's watchword was *work*,—not I dream, I purpose, or even I will do, but I *do*. He has already begun. Paul gave no countenance to that abuse of God's rich grace which encourages easy indolence and the kind of rest that does nothing because God will do all. In Paul we see a perfect example of the fine balance and proportion of character which has the most sensitive feeling, the most intense spirituality, the most devout emotion, and the most unquestioning faith, side by side with the most practical common sense." Words could not more accurately describe Dr. Simpson's own manner of life from that day forward.

Speaking at Bethshan in 1885, he said, "I have been permitted by God to work—I say this to His honor and thousands could bear witness to it—and I have worked about four times as hard as I ever did in my life. In those four years I have not had one hour away from work and have not had one single summer vacation."

For the next twelve years he continued to live in the heart of New York City in the midst of manifold ministries and constant distractions. Yet he seemed to thrive on overwork, and added burdens only increased his evident vitality.

During all the years he lived at Nyack he rarely failed to board the 6:18 A. M. train for New York City. The hour on the train was given to a rapid glance over the events of the day and to study or editorial work. Sometimes his secretary was called to his assistance on the journey. The day in New York was spent in his little office where he accomplished almost unbelievable tasks, and in interviews, in committees, and in public meetings. He was busy again on the homeward journey and, after dinner, spent hours in his study before he finally gave himself to a time of prayerful relaxation as preparation for the few hours of sleep which he allowed himself.

It is needless to recount the many activities which have been described in previous pages—his pulpit and platform work, his pastoral duties, his ministry for the sick, his lectures in the Institute, his convention tours, his correspondence, his editorial labors, his preparation of books, his production of hymns, and his executive responsibilities. For him there was no such possibility as leisure. Yet he was never flurried, even when hurrying at the last minute to keep an appointment or to catch a train. A party of friends was at the dock to bid him farewell when he was starting on his tour around the world. They sang and prayed and waited. The deck hands were loosening the tacklings when he appeared, sped up the moving gangway, turned, waved his hand and, with that ever ready wit that saved many a situation, shouted—"Goodbye; God bless you all! I'll be twenty-four hours ahead of you when I get around the world."

Yet he was never too busy to meet a special call. He had to protect himself from needless interruptions, as does every man of affairs; but when he responded, it was with rare graciousness, and few ever knew at what cost his time was given to them.

He had learned the secret of concentrating every power on the person or thing to which for the moment he gave himself, and the rarer art of a quiet dependence upon God to carry him through the hard places. To him work and communion were not antagonists but handmaidens. He expresses this in his own poetic way.

"I used to be very fond of gardening. I could work in the garden and yet smell the roses; they did not keep me from my husbandry; I had my sweet flowers every second; they did not hinder the work a bit. So you can be busy all the time, and have the breath of heaven; it will not hinder you. It is like working in a perfumed room, every sense exhilarated. It is something deeper than prayer—communion."

Dr. Simpson never sought nor expected an easy life. In one of his last public addresses he stated: "In the beginning of the life of faith God gave me a vision which to me was a symbol of the kind of life to which He had called me. In this dream a little sail boat was passing down a rapid stream, tossed by the winds and driven by the rapids. Every moment it seemed as if it must be dashed upon the rocks and crushed, yet it was preserved in some mysterious way and carried through all perils. Upon the sails of the little ship was plainly painted the name of the vessel in one Latin word, *Angustia,* meaning *Hard Places.* Through this simple dream, the Lord seemed to fortify me for the trials and testings that were ahead, and to prepare me for a life's voyage which was to be far from a smooth one, but through which God's grace would always carry me in triumph."

What was given in a vision was confirmed through the Word. In the well marked Bible which he used in his great life crisis in Louisville he heavily underscored Jeremiah 39:18, "Thy life shall be for a prey unto thee: because thou hast put thy trust in me, saith the Lord." On the margin he wrote the date, January 1, 1879, and thereafter he regarded this as one of his life texts.

When he left home for his convention tours, long or short, he carried with him work that would have overwhelmed an ordinary man, even in his office, and was always followed by numerous telegrams and piles of forwarded mail. The local demands upon him at every point were insistent; and, though he gave himself unstintedly to public service and private interviews, he usually found it necessary to resort to hotel accommodations to conserve time and strength. This was sometimes misunderstood, but here and there at least his motives were appreciated, as is shown in this incident referred to in a letter from Rev. Samuel H. Wilkinson, of the Mildmay Mission to the Jews.

"The following may seem trivial, but it reveals character. During Dr. Simpson's stay in England I invited him to take part in the Brentwood Convention. He promised to do so but stipulated that he should be accommodated at an hotel instead of in a private house because, to use his own expression, the 'social instinct' was strong in him, and he lost time and strength in conversation. I apprised him when he was to speak and named a suitable train from London. I met it on the evening he was expected and each train thereafter until almost the time of the gathering, when, leaving another to meet him at the station, I went myself to the Town Hall to apologize for Dr. Simpson's delayed arrival. But I found him there waiting for me! 'I thought,' he said, 'that I would just come down earlier in the afternoon than I was expected and sit awhile in the hotel for repose of mind.' And the incident clings even more than his splendid addresses, as an indication of the simplicity of greatness."

More of Dr. Simpson's time and energy than even intimate friends realized were spent in business affairs. In the beginning of his walk of faith he resolved that he would lead a self-supporting life. He had a large family, and the financial demands upon him as its head were constant.

His first step in this direction was taken in response to the demand for fourfold gospel literature. He decided to be his own printer, and gradually built up a plant which not only produced the books and papers which he published but later included contract work in its output. In 1912 he sold his publishing business to The Christian and Missionary Alliance, but retained his printing house, which he continued till he gave up all business affairs in 1918.

When the Missionary Institute and Berachah Home were moved to Nyack, a tract of land was purchased by a company composed of several men who had in view the establishment of an Alliance center. Their expectations in regard to a settlement on the Hillside were not fulfilled as few families made it their home. To relieve the company of its embarrassments, Dr. Simpson, who was its president, took over a large part of the lands, and this added greatly to his burdens.

Dr. Simpson also engaged in other business enterprises in New York City, not all of which were profitable. Owing to his busy life, he was obliged to commit the management to others, and his optimistic attitude toward these ventures was not always justified. Had business been his calling, some think he would have become one of the large financiers. Certainly his mind was cast in a mould that would have seemed to promise success in large undertakings.

But A. B. Simpson was called to be a prophet and not a business man. In the work which his Master appointed him and in which, in consequence, the Holy Spirit directed him, he had phenomenal success. Those who have had opportunity to know something of his affairs can also trace the loving hand of an Almighty Helper in his business life. Of this he was himself very conscious, and jottings in vest pocket note-books prove that he not only prayed but also returned thanks for God's help in his business difficulties. There is no question that his business was the great burden that finally proved too heavy for him. He would have surrendered it in his later years; but while his own strength endured, he could see no way of deliverance. When he could no longer conduct it, he acknowledged to intimate associates that he had been mistaken in entering into business and that he should have kept himself free, as did the apostles, to give himself to "prayer and to the ministry of the word."

During the Annual Council of The Christian and Missionary Alliance in May, 1918, Dr. Simpson conferred with several of his brethren in regard to his business affairs. He now felt that, as some of these interests had been closely associated with his public ministry, it would be fitting for him to entrust their settlement to the Society. It was found that there were legal difficulties in the way of such action, and after careful consideration he made a complete assignment to Mr. Franklin L. Groff, one of the oldest and most trusted business men in the Tabernacle and in the Alliance, who formed a company made up of prominent members of these organizations, to administer this trust. Through careful management of these affairs under proper legal advice, this company has been enabled by favorable disposition of his holdings, and by special supplementary gifts and pledges from friends, to provide for the liquidation of all obligations.

Dr. Simpson never accepted a salary from the Gospel Tabernacle nor even the small living allowance granted to missionaries and executive officers of The Christian and Missionary Alliance, and often refused even his traveling expenses to conventions. Regarding this relationship to his congregation, he more than once said to an associate pastor that it might be a very good school of faith for the pastor but that it was very bad discipline for the flock. When he finally relinquished his business, the Board of The Christian and Missionary Alliance gave him an ample living allowance and continues to provide similarly for Mrs. Simpson.

How fully his intense life was appreciated by men and women of every estate, and especially by the great men of action, was shown by the tributes paid to him on the platform, in the press, and in personal letters when he was called home. Several, including his old associate Dr. F. W. Farr, were reminded of the fiery prophet of Gilead and exclaimed as did Elisha—"My father, my father, the chariot of Israel, and the horsemen thereof." Mr. W. R. Moody, of Northfield, was most impressed by "the faithfulness of his Christian stewardship," and adds, "Untiring in his labors, unsparing of his time, he wore himself out in the service of his Master." Dr. Geo. H. Sandison, Editor of *The Christian Herald,* wrote: "I can think of no one in this age who has done more effective, self-denying service for Christ and His Gospel than Albert B. Simpson." "His missionary zeal was astounding," said his old friend, Dr. George F. Pentecost; and with this agrees another associate of other days, Dean Arthur C. Peck, who testifies that "his labors were apostolic in both spirit and scope. No man ever wrought more abundantly and successfully among the heathen." He was "fully absorbed in the missionary enterprise and devoted all his energies to hasten the coming of the King," is the impression left upon Rev. J. M. Pike, Editor of the *Way of Faith*. "I remember," said Pastor P. W. Philpott at the memorial service, "reading a letter from a boy to his mother during the days of war, in which he said, 'You know it is not how long a man lives that counts; it is what he puts into life while he is living.' And if that is true, Dr. Simpson has lived about three times longer than any other man of his age, for he surely put into the last thirty years three times as much as the ordinary minister."

There must have been some great secret hidden from ordinary ken, some springs of action and fountains of energy that accounted for such a life. Here he reveals one of them. "There is no service which God expects of us for which He has not made the fullest provision in the infinite resources of His grace. We cannot dare too much if it be in dependence upon Him, for He has given us all His fullness, and sends no one warring upon His own charges." The following quotation suggests another secret. "The power to serve God is no natural talent or acquired experience, but Christ's own life and power in us through the Holy Ghost. And no man can serve God without the Spirit." And yet another is disclosed in a stanza from one of his poems:

> "I dwell with the King for His work,
>   And the work, it is His and not mine;
> He plans and prepares it for me
>   And fills me with power divine.
> So duty is changed to delight,
>   And prayer into praise as I sing;
> I dwell with my King for His work
>   And work in the strength of my King."

Further, Dr. Simpson's attitude to life was that of the Son of man who "came not to be ministered unto but to minister." "What," he says, "would we think of Jesus if we ever found Him looking for His own pleasure or consulting His own comfort?" And yet again, he had felt the pulse of the times for he says: "Everything around us is intensely alive; life is earnest; death is earnest; sin is earnest; men are earnest; business is earnest; knowledge is earnest; the age is earnest; God forgive *us* if we alone are trifling in the white heat of this crisis time." This conception moved him to write one of his most stirring poems:

"No time for trifling in this life of mine;
　　Not this the path the blessed Master trod,
　But strenuous toil; each hour and power employed
　　Always and all for God.

"Time swiftly flies; eternity is near,
　　And soon my dust may lie beneath the sod.
　How dare I waste my life or cease to be
　　Always and all for God!

"I catch the meaning of this solemn age;
　　With life's vast issues all my soul is awed.
　Life was not given for trifling; it must be
　　Always and all for God.

"I hear the footfalls of God's mighty hosts
　　Whom God is sending all the earth abroad;
　Like them let me be busy for His cause,
　　Always and all for God."

There was to him a motive power in "The Blessed Hope." He sings "Let us live in the light of His coming," and in the following stanza he reveals his sense of responsibility:

"Hasting on the coming of the Master,
　　Let us speed the days that linger still;

> Time is counted yonder, not by numbers,
>   But conditions which we may fulfil.
> If we bring the "other sheep" to Jesus,
>   If we send the Gospel everywhere,
> We may hasten forward His appearing,
>   And His blessed coming help prepare."

Not the least of these secrets was a right apprehension of God. One night, after he had been meditating on the ways of some modern "Quietists," he fell asleep and dreamed that he saw an office immensely larger than any he had ever conceived. God was in the midst of it and radiating from Him were visible electric waves which reached the uttermost parts of the earth, everywhere creating intense activity but without confusion or strain. The impression left upon him when he awoke of God's omnipresence and omnipotence was lasting. Thereafter, even more than before, he was encouraged to "attempt great things for God."

CHAPTER 17

A PAULINE MYSTIC

S OMEONE with a true conception of mysticism and an intimate knowledge of A. B. Simpson has called him "the last of the great mystics." From first to last his life is a mystery if viewed from rationalistic ground. A mystic by hereditary temperament, a Celtic facility for seeing the invisible struggled for the mastery of his youthful soul against the cold logic of ultra-Calvinism. Who can read the self revelation he has given in his reminiscences of his conversion without sympathetic pangs? There came a day after years of soul agony when the veil was rent, and he was ushered into the fellowship of the true mystics of the ages, thenceforth, like Moses, to endure "as seeing him who is invisible."

Some of Dr. Simpson's friends express dissent when he is referred to as a mystic, evidently because of very general misconceptions of what mysticism is. These are very clearly summarized by Professor W. K. Fleming in *Mysticism in Christianity*. "We find three accusations quite commonly brought against mysticism—that it deals in unsafe and presumptuous speculation; or that it encourages a sort of extravagant, unhealthy, hysterical self-hypnotism; or that it is merely quasi-spiritual feeling, vague, dreamy, and unpractical."

The same writer replies that mysticism is not equivalent merely to symbolism; that it has nothing whatever to do with occult pursuits, magic, and the like, although some have lost their way and floundered into this particular

morass; that it has no connection with miracle working
and the like; that although mystics have frequently had
visions, mysticism is not a dreaming of dreams nor dreami-
ness at all; and indeed that mystics have more commonly
than not been known as very practical men and women.

What then is mysticism? Ewald says "it is the craving
to be united with God." Professor Seth Pringle-Pattison
sees that, to the mystic, "God ceases to be an object and
becomes an experience." Professor Harnack writes that
"Mysticism is rationalism applied to a sphere above reason"; and Dean Inge, who perhaps is the clearest exponent of this subject, makes Harnack's statement read,
"Mysticism is reason applied to a sphere above rationalism." This fairly well defines the subject in general, but
stops far short of Pauline mysticism.

Some writers have attempted to classify mystics into
extreme mystics, who disregard everything but their
revelations; *super-rational mystics* who, regarding ordinary Christian experience as merely preliminary to mystical communion, are indifferent to the externals of doctrine, worship, and sacraments; and *rational mystics* who
would agree with Dean Inge. If such a classification
were complete, such men as Dr. Simpson would necessarily be included in the last class.

Within the orthodox fold a distinction is sometimes
made between the mystical and the evangelical method,
the mystic reaching truth through internal experience of
Christ, while the evangelical attains it by historic fact—
"the Christ picture presented to the mind by gospel history." Dr. Simpson was both truly mystical and thoroughly evangelical. So were the apostles and so are
some of the great men of our day. Therefore we
need a better classification, and recognizing this, we

may safely say that A. B. Simpson was one of the
school of *evangelical mystics*.

Some have charged mystics with pessimism, forgetting
that every prophet to a sterile age and a backslidden people is of necessity pessimistic concerning his times and
his compatriots. So were the Hebrew prophets regarded.
"Which of the prophets have not your fathers perse-
cuted?" asked Stephen of his own generation. But the
prophet and the mystic are eventually optimists. They
see their own times clearly because they have seen all
time, and eternity, and God Himself. The mystic mounts
up as a seer on wings like eagles; runs the race of a man
without being weary; and walks the rugged, thorny pathway of earth without fainting because he waits upon the
Lord. The Pauline mystic is always mightier than the
materialist and more practical, for men must always
dream dreams before they blaze new trails and see visions
before they are strong to do exploits.

There was a medieval mysticism which shut men up
in the cloister, and there is still an abnormal mysticism of
certain Christian sects. But there remains today a pure
mysticism which was the very breath and life of Biblical
Judaism, and which is the secret of the real power of the
Church. Without this mysticism there never would have
been a reformation or a revival. It was a revelation that
saved Noah; a voice that called Abraham; a burning bush
that transformed Moses; a vision that inspired Isaiah; a
call that strengthened Jeremiah; and a visitation of the
Son of God that recreated Saul of Tarsus. Augustine,
Luther, Calvin, Knox, Wesley, Edwards, and Finney
were scholars and philosophers, but it was a knowledge of
the mysteries of God that made them mightier than prel-
acies, thrones, and universities.

It was time for another mystic to appear. Mists hung in our valleys of experience, and clouds enveloped our mountains of vision. We were threatened with a creedless Church, a Christless education, and a powerless religion. Men were wearying for some one to lead them directly to God, and A. B. Simpson was God's man for the hour.

The word *mysterion*, which is used in the New Testament of divine mysteries, is derived from *mystes*, meaning one who was initiated into divine things. But while the Greek mystic was initiated into the secret circle of the oracle and must keep his mouth shut—as the root meaning of the verbal form indicates—the Christian mystic was given a glorious revelation of things which he was to declare. Paul and John indeed heard and saw some things which they could not disclose, but the mysteries of divine grace were given to them on the terms stated by Jesus, "What I tell you in the darkness, speak ye in the light; and what ye hear in the ear, proclaim upon the housetops." (A.S.V.)

These mysteries include the whole heritage of the revelation manifested to the patriarchs and to the prophets of Israel, and which was more perfectly revealed in and through Christ and to His apostles. Those clearly specified in the New Testament are the mystery of God, of God's wisdom, of Christ, of the incarnation, of the Gospel, of faith, of Christ in you, of the body of Christ, of the fellow-heirship of the Gentiles, of our inheritance in Christ, of iniquity, of the rapture, of Israel, of the kingdom, and of its capture from Satan.

Pauline mysticism included all of these and to him all of them were essential; yet it is on those mysteries which pertain to Christ Himself, whom he had hated, that he loved to dwell. He never recovered from the marvel that to him, the persecutor, Christ should appear in person and make him the recipient of some of these mysteries.

When we speak of A. B. Simpson as a Pauline mystic we mean that he followed Paul in his comprehension and declaration of the divine mysteries. With the history of Christian mysticism and its errors he was conversant, but he escaped the pitfalls in this path by overleaping them and going directly to Jesus and John and Paul for his teaching. And herein he was an evangelical mystic. The same safeguard enabled him to pass unscathed through a veritable vortex of current mysticism. He was continually beset both by interviews and through correspondence by extremists and faddists. Some of the leaders of modern movements would have plucked out their right eye to make him a disciple. But he kept his own course, and that always held right onward to the fullness of Christ.

He was Pauline in his emphasis. Perhaps no modern teacher had so well-rounded a theology or was so safe a guide in all the mysteries of revelation. But, while he dealt simply and fearlessly with every revealed mystery, he dwelt most upon the great mystery which had been specially revealed to Paul—"Christ in you, the hope of glory," whom he, like Paul, preached, "warning every man, and teaching every man in all wisdom; that we may present every man perfect in Christ Jesus."

He was Pauline in his simplicity. It is only those who try to peer through a curtain who speak in riddles of what they see. Those who have been behind the veil come forth to tell in simple terms what has been revealed to them. A child can follow him in this passage from his great sermon, "Himself." "That word, *mystery,* means secret. It is the great secret. And I can tell you today, nay, I can give you—if you will take it from Him, not from me—a secret which has been to me, O, so wonderful! A good many years ago I came to Him burdened with guilt and fear; I took that simple secret, and it took away all my fear and sin. Years passed on, and I found sin overcame me and my temptations were too strong for me. I came to Him a second time, and He whispered to me, 'Christ in you,' and I had victory, rest, and such sweet blessing ever since; for more than twelve years it has been so precious."

This central truth of Paul's message needed to be restated and revived in the Church. As conservative a teacher as Dr. MacLaren, of Manchester, said, "This great truth, the indwelling Christ, is practically lost to the Church. To me this truth, Christ in me and I in Christ, is the very heart of Christianity, for which Christ for us is the preface and introduction. You may call it mysticism if you like. There is no grasp of the deepest things in religion without that which the irreligious mind thinks it has disposed of by the cheap and easy sneer that it is mystical." No man since the days of Paul has done more to make this vital truth of Christian life real and practical in the Church than A. B. Simpson. Had he done nothing else and nothing more, he still would live as one of the greatest men of the age.

Paul's mysticism was crystallized in the phrase, "Christ in you, the hope of glory." This became the very heart of A. B. Simpson's message.

> "This is my wonderful story;
>   Christ to my heart has come;
> Jesus, the King of glory,
>   Finds in my heart a home."

Inseparable from this in Jesus' teaching and in the Pauline doctrine is the other mystery, "in Christ." The two are one in Dr. Simpson's experience and expression. He thus concludes the hymn quoted,

> "Now in His bosom confiding,
>   This my glad song shall be,
> I am in Jesus abiding;
>   Jesus abides in me."

This mystic union with Christ appears in every phase of his teaching. Salvation is not the outcome of faith in a mere historic fact, but identification with Christ in His very death.

> "I am crucified with Jesus,
>   And the Cross hath set me free;
> I have risen again with Jesus,
>   And He lives and reigns in me.
>
> "Mystery hid from ancient ages
>   But at length to faith made plain,
> Christ in me, the Hope of Glory;
>   Tell it o'er and o'er again."

Perhaps none of the mystics since John and Paul have approached him in his daring assumption of the rights of redemption, and nowhere has he made so bold in his utterance as in his hymn, "Even As He." If it were not true, it would be blasphemy; but some one printed it on a leaflet and sent it broadcast with a scripture reference to every line, the application of which was indisputable. It begins,

> "Oh, what a wonderful place
>   Jesus has given to me!
> Saved by His glorious grace,
>   I may be even as He.

> "When with my Lord I appear,
>   Like Him I know I shall be;
> But while I walk with Him here,
>   I may be even as He."

And so the hymn sweeps on through all of the experiences through which our living Head passed, from the cradle to the coronation, claiming everywhere our right of identification with Him.

To him the coming of the Lord was not so much an event as a Person, an eternal and inseparable union with Christ.

> "Some sweet hour our mortal frame
>   Shall His glorious image wear;
> Some sweet hour our worthless name
>   All His majesty shall share."

Naturally we have turned to Dr. Simpson's poems, because poetry is both the gift and the expression of mysticism. His prose writings, however, are quite as rich. After his life crisis, it seemed impossible for him to preach a sermon or write an article which was not permeated with the mysteries of the Gospel.

The effect upon his ministry is revealed in a confession which he makes in *The Fulness of Jesus.* "I am always ashamed to say it, but it is true, that in the years that I did not know Christ as an indwelling Spirit in my heart, I never had a single Christian come to speak to me about their spiritual life. I was a pastor for ten years before this, and in all those ten years I seldom had a Christian come to me and say, 'Dear pastor, I want you to tell me how to enter into a deeper Christian life.' I had sinners come because I knew something about forgiveness, and so I could preach to them. But the very moment that God came into my heart and gave me this indwelling

Christ, the hungry Christians began to come to me; and from that time, for years, hundreds have come to be helped to find the Lord as a personal indwelling life and power.

So, too, he found in this the secret of Christian unity. He writes in *Words of Comfort for Tried Ones:* "It is as we are united to Him that we are attached to each other, and all Christian unity depends upon oneness with the Lord. The secret of Christian union is not platforms, creeds, or even cooperative work, but it is one life, one heart, one spirit, in the fellowship and love of Jesus Christ."

He escaped controversy and became a great reconciling force in theology by holding to this mystical treatment of the great issues. His most widely circulated and most God-honored tract, "Himself," was an impromptu address given at the Bethshan Conference in 1885 on an afternoon when the most conflicting theories of sanctification had been assertively proclaimed. Referring to it years afterwards, he said, "We were delighted to find at the close of the services that all parties could unite in this testimony and around this common center."

He discovered that power is not committed to us, but communicated through this mystic union, and states this simply in *The Sweetest Christian Life.* "Let us carefully note that this power is all centered in a Person, namely, the living Christ. It is not so much power communicated to him to be at his own control and disposal as a dynamo or battery might be; but the power remains in the Person of Christ and is only shared by him while he is in direct union and communion with the Lord Himself."

To him it was the secret of the overcoming life. Thousands have read this passage from his book of morning devotions, *Days of Heaven upon Earth*. "A precious secret of Christian life is to have Jesus dwelling within and conquering things that we never could overcome. It is the only secret of power in your life and mine. Men cannot understand it, nor will the world believe it, but it is true that God will come and dwell within us, and be the power and the purity and the victory and the joy of our life."

He saw the weakness in Thomas a Kempis' presentation, *Imitation of Christ,* and we find him writing: "It is Christ Himself who comes to imitate Himself in us and reproduce His own life in the lives of His followers. This is the mystery of the Gospel. This is the secret of the Lord. This is the power that sanctifies, that fills, that keeps the consecrated heart. This is the only way that we can be like Christ."

He also felt keenly the lack in some of the schools of holiness, as this terse statement shows. "Even the teachers of holiness are in danger of substituting it for Him, a clean heart for the divine nature. The mystery of godliness is Christ in you the hope of glory. The end of all experience is union with God." Nevertheless, he goes far beyond these teachers, for he says, "Redemption is not the restoration of fallen man, but the new creation of a redeemed family under the headship of the second Adam, on an infinitely higher plane than even unfallen humanity could ever have reached alone. We are first born of Christ, and then united to Him, just as Eve was formed out of her husband and then wedded to him. So the redeemed soul is formed out of the Saviour and then united to Him in an everlasting bond of love and unity, more intimate than any human relationship can ever express."

Nor would he give ground to those teachers who make the terms of intimate union used in the New Testament mere figures. "This is not a beautiful figure of speech, but it is a real visitation of God. I wonder if we know what this means. Does it seem an awful thing to have God visit us? My idea of it used to be that it would kill a person. It would be more than he could stand. And yet it is represented in God's Word as an actual visitation. Christ is not to be an outside influence which moves on our emotions and feelings and elevates us into a sublime idea of God, but the real presence of Christ has come within us to remain, and He brings with Him all His resources of help and love and mighty power."

No one who knows Dr. Simpson's life would accuse him of holding the errors of *Quietism*. Yet in one of his most widely scattered leaflets, *The Power of Stillness,* he confesses that from the Quietists he learned a truth which was one of the secrets of his life. "A score of years ago a friend placed in my hand a little book which led me to one of the turning points in my life. It was an old medieval message, and it had but one thought and it was this, that God was waiting in the depth of my being to talk with me if I would only get still enough to hear Him.

"I thought that this would be a very easy matter, so I began to get still. But I had no sooner commenced than a perfect pandemonium of voices reached my ears, a thousand clamoring notes from without and within, until I could hear nothing but their noise and their din. Some of them were my own questions, some of them my own cares, some of them my own prayers. Others were the suggestions of the tempter and the voices of the world's turmoil. Never before did there seem so many things to be done, to be said, to be thought; and in every direction I was pulled, and pushed, and greeted with noisy acclamations and unspeakable unrest. It seemed necessary for me to listen to some of them, but God said, 'Be still and know that I am God.' Then came the conflict of thoughts for the morrow, and its duties and cares, but God said, 'Be still.'

"And as I listened and slowly learned to obey and shut my ears to every sound, I found that after a while, when the other voices ceased or I ceased to hear them, there was a still, small voice in the depth of my spirit. As I listened, it became to me the power of prayer and the voice of wisdom and the call of duty, and I did not need to think so hard, or pray so hard, or trust so hard, but that still, small voice of the Holy Spirit in my heart was God's prayer in my secret soul and God's answer to all my questions."

He had also learned that the secret of maintaining this union with Christ is the mystery of faith. "It means staying in God. When the dear Lord led me into this place, I entered it without any feeling whatever, and simply trusted Him for everything. But after several months I found there was a great change in my feelings. Then I immediately turned around and trusted the change and became happy and buoyant because I was changed. It completely uprooted my faith. I had taken up the little plant of trust from the soil God meant it to live in and planted it in a hot-bed of my own preparing, and, of course, it died. Ah, how many trust in their own feelings or their own altered circumstances! This is not abiding in Christ."

Such a life was the ideal which he held before him for his spiritual children. To an extent that perhaps he never dared to hope his desire has been realized not only in his own congregation and the numberless persons who crowded the great conventions, but also far away in heathen lands. There has arisen a church, an elect of God from among all nations, whose enlightened eyes have seen things invisible and whose hearts burn with something of Paul's passion to declare the mystery of the Gospel, even though it should lead them, as it did the Apostle, to prison and to bonds.

CHAPTER 18

A MAN OF PRAYER

S OME one who wished to discover the secret of the life of Bengel hid himself in his study to see and hear him pray. After hours of work upon his commentary the saintly student rose, looked upward, and said, "Lord Jesus Christ, things stand with us on the old terms."

If we are to know Dr. Simpson, we must reverently approach his prayer closet. We may be as greatly surprised as was Bengel's friend, for every mystic has learned the simplicity and the continuity of prayer.

Prayer is one of the mysteries. In his discussion of the supernatural in *Present Truth* Dr. Simpson says, "There is no wonder more supernatural and divine in the life of the believer than the mystery and the ministry of prayer . . . wonder of wonders! Mystery of mysteries! Miracle of miracles! The hand of the child touching the arm of the Father and moving the wheels of the universe. Beloved, this is your supernatural place and mine, and over its gates we read the inspiring invitation, 'Thus saith the Lord . . . Call unto me, and I will answer thee, and shew thee great and mighty things, which thou knowest not'."

This promise, given to Jeremiah, was Dr. Simpson's great life text, and became the foundation of that daring faith which was the secret of his mighty ministry. It led him to exhort us to "see that our highest ministry and power is to deal with God for men" and to believe that "our highest form of service is the ministry of prayer."

Dr. Simpson had solved the secret of service when he learned the mystery of prayer. In prayer he received a vision of God's will. Through further prayer he ascertained God's plans for the carrying out of His will. Still praying, he was empowered to execute those plans. More prayer brought the supply of every need for the work. Continuing still in prayer, he was able to carry through what he had begun. Praying always, a spirit of praise and adoration welled up in his heart, and God received all the glory for everything that was accomplished.

To Dr. Simpson prayer was not an exercise or a ritual, but a life. In the introduction to *The Life of Prayer* he exclaims: "The Life of Prayer! Great and sacred theme! It leads us into the Holy of Holies and the secret place of the Most High. It is the very life of the Christian, and it touches the very life of God Himself."

This life of prayer was to him a phase of the Spirit-filled life. We find him writing, "The Holy Ghost is the source and substance of all that prayer can ask, and a gift that carries with it the pledge of all other gifts and blessings. In the parallel passages in Matthew and Luke "the Holy Spirit" and "all good things" are synonymous. He that has the Holy Spirit shall have all good things. And again we read, "Praying in the Holy Ghost means simply this: When the Holy Ghost comes in, He comes as a living Person and takes charge of the whole life, planning for us, watching over us, fitting into every need for every moment, for there is not a moment when He is not trying to pray in us some prayer."

Though he knew that faith is essential in true prayer and emphasized this, he also knew that "we will not have much of the divine element of holy faith in us unless we feed it day by day with prayer. We must live a life of constant prayer." He often quoted Montgomery's lines:

> "Prayer is the Christian's vital breath
> The Christian's native air."

Prayer, as Dr. Simpson came to understand it, was one of the expressions of union with Christ. He liked to refer to Dr. Robert E. Speer's remark to a friend that normal Christian living is the attitude of mind and heart that reverts immediately to consciousness of Christ when released from absorbing affairs. In one of the issues of the *Tabernacle Sermons* where the indwelling of Christ is vividly presented, this personal experience is given: "I go back in memory this morning to the time when He first came to me in this way and taught me to trust His presence and lean in prayer upon Him every moment. I came to realize it quietly, for there was nothing startling about it. Day after day the consciousness became clearer that God was here. I did not have to mount up to the sky to find Him. I never whispered to Him but He answered, 'Here am I.' Oh, how precious it is to be overshadowed thus by the cloud of His presence."

So to him prayer was a habit of life, a free companionship with an almighty, omniscient, omnipresent Friend. In one of his books for daily devotion, he gave us this counsel: "An important help in the life of prayer is the habit of bringing everything to God, moment by moment, as it comes to us in life." He had found that the command "Pray without ceasing" meant that we were to make request "for such things as we need in our common life from day to day. This is, after all, the real secret of constant prayer. In no other way can we intelligently pray without ceasing without stepping aside from the path of daily duty and neglecting the callings of life and the obligations of our various situations. There are very few that can spend an entire day, and none that can devote every day and every hour to abstract devotion and internal communion with God about things quite removed from the ordinary things of life; and, even if this could be done, it would simply develop monasticism, which has never been a wholesome type of Christian experience. It needs the coloring of actual life to give vitality, reality, and practical force to our communion with God."

His confidence in prayer was rooted in his knowledge of the immeasurable reaches of redemption, and because of this he could not only ask boldly himself but lead others to ask and receive. When a young lady came to his office to ask him to pray for her, he finally solved her perplexities by saying, "Suppose a friend were to deposit $100 at Macy's and say 'I want you to get whatever you wish', but you were to say, 'Mr. Macy, I would not dare to buy a hundred dollars' worth'. Would he not say, 'The money is paid and is to your credit; you are very foolish if you do not get the benefit of it.' That is the way we go to God. We have nothing to present to Him as a claim, but on the books of God the infinite righteousness of Christ has been deposited to our credit, and God comes and says: 'In His name ask My help as far as that credit will go.' You have not any right, but He has the right, and He gives it to you. 'Oh,' said the young lady, 'I see it. Why, I think I could ask God for anything now'."

Some say that we should ask once for a thing and leave it with God; not so Dr. Simpson. "What did Paul do? The right thing. He prayed and prayed and prayed. So should you. It is all right to pray and to pray again and to pray yet again and to pray until God answers you. Paul prayed until God answered him. He said, 'Paul, I have to disappoint you. I am not going to take this thorn away'." How sanely he presented this in one of his Friday meeting talks. "Probably this is the best rule about prayer: to pray until we understand the mind of the Lord about it, and get sufficient light, direction, and comfort to satisfy our hearts. There is such a thing as vain repetition, and there is such a thing as supplication and continuance in prayer. The Spirit must guide rightly in each case, but a heaven-taught heart will pray until it cannot pray any more. As soon as the assurance comes, we should stop praying, and henceforth everything should be praise."

Deeper than his own consciousness there was in Dr. Simpson's life what he calls "wordless prayer." He speaks of this in *Days of Heaven.* "In the consecrated believer the Holy Spirit is preeminently a Spirit of prayer. If our whole being is committed to Him, and our thoughts are at His bidding, He will occupy every moment in communion and occupy everything as it comes, and we shall pray it out in our spiritual consciousness before we act it out in our lives. We shall, therefore, find ourselves taking up the burdens of life and praying them out in a wordless prayer which we ourselves often cannot understand, but which is simply the unfolding of His thought and will within us, and which will be followed by the unfolding of His providence concerning us."

This unbroken fellowship was maintained by definite communion and intercession. It was Dr. Simpson's habit to spend a time, after he had laid his work aside each night, in unhindered, conscious fellowship with Christ. He called it his love life, and it was as real to him as the interchange of thought and feeling between the most devoted lovers. It was his daily renewal of life, his rest before sleep, his outgiving of worship and adoration, and his inbreathing of the very fullness of God. When for a little time this fellowship, unbroken for years, was clouded, he was like a weaned child, and those who had the privilege of intimacy with him in the last months of his life can never forget his satisfaction when his wearied brain found abiding rest in the restored consciousness of the continuous presence of his Lord.

Such was his life of fellowship. But his closet prayer was more than communion. "Perhaps," he says, "the highest ministry of prayer is for others." He knew the meaning of a "burden" of prayer. He carried his congregation, his world-wide constituency, but most of all his missionaries in his heart. Sometimes when an overwhelming burden was upon him for some far-away missionary, it would be explained by a cable calling for prayer for this very person. The various departments of the many-sided work, his private business concerns, his family and personal friends called for continual intercession.

How pressing were those demands for prayer no one but he and his Lord ever knew, for he treated his prayer life as confidential business with God. In his vest pocket diary were found memos of these needs, sometimes for his children, at other times for his associates, and often for financial demands. An ejaculatory prayer such as "Thou knowest, Lord," usually followed. Very frequently on the same date, or soon after, was written some such grateful acknowledgment as "Praise God, need met!"

His testings of faith were often severe. In a record of the early days in New York he frankly acknowledged that: "The pastor receives no salary whatever, nor a single penny from the ordinary revenues of the church. From the first he placed all he had at God's service and trusted

Him alone for himself and family. He has no private means whatever, but the wants of his family are daily supplied by the providential care of God. Often when there was nothing left and when no mortal dreamed of their need, God has prompted some heart to call or send exactly the amount required."

An incident recalled by Mrs. Simpson bears out his statement. "We had moved from the comfortable Manse on Thirty-second Street to a little four-room apartment. One morning we had nothing for breakfast but oatmeal. Not being able to trust the Lord as my husband was doing, I went out and for the first time in my life ordered supplies for which I could not pay. For some days Mr. Simpson received very little money. Sometimes he would come in with a small piece of meat or some other necessity. One morning I received a letter from a lady in Philadelphia, whom I did not know, containing a check for one hundred and fifty dollars. I hurried over to the church office to have Mr. Simpson cash it at a neighboring bank, and then made the rounds of the stores to pay the bills. That was the first and last time I ever bought anything for which I could not pay."

This life of intercession was the secret of his successful public ministry. No one knew this so well as he, for in *The King's Business* he says: "I have noticed that those who claim and expect souls for God have them given to them; and, for myself, I never dare to preach to the unsaved without first claiming alone with God the real birth of souls, and receiving the assurance of His quickening and new-creating life distinctly for this end. If I fail to do this, I am usually disappointed in the results of the meeting."

His private prayer life also explains the power that

Dr. Simpson had in public prayer and in intercession with individuals. Who can forget the prayers he offered in his pulpit or the petitions which he poured forth as he knelt beside some needy soul? Rev. Kenneth Mackenzie aptly expresses our feeling: "My memory recalls most vividly his unction in prayer. Though I hated to have to encroach upon him for this ministry, I never came away from his presence without a deepened sense of the nearness of the Lord. No one can describe that power which he so charmingly expressed as he poured out his soul in unselfish importunity for others. It would be sacrilegious to try. But thousands have known it and blessed God for it."

Mrs. A. A. Kirk, who for some years was associated with Dr. Simpson in the Missionary Institute, recalls that on the occasion of her first meeting with him he prayed "Oh, Lord, may she be the mother of a thousand," and that undreamed of enlargement of ministry came to her. She is but one of hundreds who look back to a moment when a Spirit-inspired prayer breathed through him by the Spirit of God opened the gates into a life of ministry in the power of the Highest.

On one occasion Dr. Simpson was holding a convention in the Scranton Valley. A child was dying of diphtheria in one of the Alliance families, and threats were being made against the parents and Rev. W. T. MacArthur. After the evening meeting Mr. MacArthur told Mr. Simpson of the circumstances and asked him to go to see the child. Together they knelt at the little bedside. "It seemed," says Mr. MacArthur, "as if a great giant had stooped his shoulders under an insuperable burden. But it presently began to give way, and we were all lifted up into the very presence of God. Then he said, 'Now,

Mac, you pray.' But there was nothing to pray for. We all knew that the child was healed, and when the physician came in the morning, his mouth was stopped."

How aptly he would turn everything into fuel for the fires of prayer is shown by an illustration in his first missionary magazine *The Gospel in All Lands*. "I will kill you," said a gentleman on the deck of a vessel, as he held a pistol to the head of a workman by his side, "I will kill you on the spot if you stop those bellows for a single second; my brother is down in that diving-bell; that tube must supply him with the air he breathes every moment, and you hold his breath in your hands. Be steady'." Then he compared this to "holding in our hands by believing prayer the vital breath of men and women who have gone down into the engulfing waves of heathenism, while we close the tube, drop the bellows, and forget their desperate need." He also used it in one of his most pathetic missionary hymns, the first verse of which reads

"Down amid the depths of heathen darkness
  There are heroes true and brave;
Shrinking not from death, or toil, or danger,
  They have gone to help and save.
But we hear them crying, 'Do not leave us
  Mid these dreadful depths to drown;
Let us feel your arms of pray'r around us;
  Hold the ropes as we go down'."

Many of his sweetest hymns were born in prayer and lift us as his own heart was lifted into the very presence of God in intercession, aspiration, adoration and praise. Some have even felt that they must cease to pray as they followed him into the heights and depths of his passionate prayer life. Who of us was not humbled when he first read:

"O Love that gave itself for me,
  Help me to love and live like Thee,
And kindle in this heart of mine
  The passion fire of love divine.

"Set all my ransomed powers on fire;
  Give me the love that naught can tire,
And kindle in this heart of mine
  The living fire of zeal divine.

"O Holy Ghost, for Thee I cry;
  Baptize with power from on high,
And kindle in this heart of mine
  The living fire of power divine.

"Help me to pray till all my soul
  Shall move and bend at Thy control,
And kindle in this heart of mine,
  The living fire of power divine."

With such a leader the Alliance could not but be a prayer movement. It was born in the soul agony of a man who had seen a vision and had paid the price of his dream. It has been nourished on prayer. His desire to keep it simple and always dependent upon the Lord was a passion. When he could no longer preach or use his pen, he prayed night and day for his spiritual children and for the great purpose into which they had been called. While we pray as he prayed, we shall continue to carry on the work which God gave him to do and which is left for us to finish.

CHAPTER 19

A MODERN PROPHET

WHEN we speak of a modern prophet, some will take it as an epithet applied in eulogy, an exaggeration of a preacher's gifts for the sake of effect. Others will question our point of view, for there is a very widespread notion that there are no prophets today. The popular idea is that prophets lived in Bible times and predicted coming events. On the other hand the rationalistic wing of the modern school regards the prophet as a statesman and reformer dealing with the social, political, ethical and religious problems of his time, and that there is no essential difference between the prophets of the Bible and men of this type today. Both of these views are imperfect and misleading.

The Bible is very definite as to the nature of the prophetic office. God said to Abimelech concerning Abraham, "He is a prophet, and he shall pray for thee, and thou shalt live" (Gen. 20:7). When Moses complained about his slowness of speech, God said, Aaron "shall be thy spokesman unto the people; and it shall come to pass, that he shall be to thee a mouth, and thou shalt be to him as God." (A.S.V.) Before he spoke to Pharaoh Jehovah said unto Moses, "See, I have made thee as God to Pharaoh: and Aaron thy brother shall be thy prophet." (A.S.V.)

These earliest references show that there are three parties to prophecy—God, man and a mediator who can speak to each party for the other. Thus we find Haggai the prophet describing himself as "Jehovah's messenger in Jehovah's message'" (A.S.V.)—a simpler definition of a prophet cannot be given. The subject matter of the message may be disregarded, for it matters not whether the message concerns the physical or the spiritual in man or whether it regards the present or the future. The all-important factors are that the prophet be in actual communication with God, and that he has been given a message to communicate.

The office was continued in the New Testament dispensation. Paul wrote to the Ephesians that when Christ ascended on high, He gave gifts unto men; "And he gave some to be apostles; and some, prophets; and some, evangelists; and some, pastors and teachers; for the perfecting of the saints, unto the work of ministering, unto the building up of the body of Christ." (A.S.V.) Until the Body, the Church, is complete, these gifts will continue.

"Desire earnestly to prophesy" Paul says to the Corinthians. "He that prophesieth speaketh unto men edification, and exhortation, and consolation." (A.S.V.) The teacher teaching the Word of God, the evangelist telling out the glad tidings of salvation, the pastor shepherding the flock are not necessarily prophets; for the prophet, whether as a teacher he edifies, as an evangelist he exhorts, or as a pastor he consoles his people, has come out of the inner chamber of God's presence with a specific message for a special occasion. Any one who has received this gift of prophecy may properly be called a modern prophet.

It was this mystical element in Dr. Simpson's later ministry, this prophetic office to which he was called, that made him more than a great pulpiteer, evangelist, and pastor—he was all these in his early ministry. Now he was lifted into the circle of those to whom are committed the oracles of God.

The biographer of Lucius B. Compton, the mountain evangelist, says that many have gone miles to hear Compton only to be greatly disappointed; but that when God had a message to give to men, and had chosen Lucius B. Compton to declare it, no one was ever disappointed. This is his way of saying that God had taken an ignorant, stammering, mountain boy and at times made him a prophet. In Mr. Simpson's case God chose one whom he had already equipped with many of the spiritual gifts and graces. And furthermore his spiritual communion with God was so continuous that he seldom if ever appeared in the pulpit without a message which hearers recognized as from God.

Strange as it may seem, Balaam the soothsayer was on at least one occasion a prophet of Jehovah. But no man of any age ever exercises the prophetic gift as the sphere of his ministry who has not made a definite and complete surrender to God. Dr. Simpson clearly recognized this. "I have," he says, "often seen sermons in print that were excellent in conception, in division, in language, in illustration, and in logic, but lacking in spiritual aroma. They were cold and intellectual. When I find souls surrendered to God, I feel communion with them in what they say. The fact of their abandonment to God produces spiritual feeling, and no person can counterfeit it. Preaching without spiritual aroma is like a rose without fragrance. We can only get the perfume by getting more of Christ."

Surrender is initial but is not in itself sufficient. The prophet must walk with God. One of the Bible synonyms was "the man of God." Rev. W. T. MacArthur said of Dr. Simpson in his memorial message: "If God was his method of life, the same was true of his service. How often have I heard him say, 'I am no good unless I can get alone with God.' His practice was to hush his spirit and literally cease to think. Then in the silence of his soul he listened for 'the still, small voice.' It was thus he received his messages. Jotting down the divisions and the headings of his subjects, he was prepared either to go into his pulpit and extemporize or into his study and write." Another intimate ministerial friend says, "His immediate leaning upon the Lord for his message was a delightful study to me."

How dependent upon the Holy Spirit this master of the art of sermon building became and continued to the end of his life is shown by a conversation with Rev. R. R. Brown shortly before his ministry ended. "One day while relating some experiences in connection with the Lord's dealing with us concerning our messages, he said that he was passing through a new experience. For some time the Lord had been withholding the message he was to give, oftentimes until he entered the meeting or a few hours before at the longest. He continued his study and research but contrary to his habits the Holy Spirit had been teaching him new lessons of waiting and trusting for the message."

In an informal address to the class in homiletics in the Missionary Institute, when he had been fifty-one years in the ministry, he told them that he had spent his birthday on the hill-top seeking some new enduement for service and had received a renewed call both to studious preparation and prayerful reception of his messages.

In his conception of preaching, such studious preparation and prayerful reception of the message were not contradictory terms. Dean Turnbull has written: "He was a scholar of profound and varied learning, who could countenance no mental shallowness or inadequate standards in teaching. He believed that the minister of God should be not only spiritually equipped but also as well developed intellectually as opportunity would permit. His faith in God's ability to quicken the mind and to thoroughly equip those who would not be considered qualified according to ordinary educational standards has been amply justified by the achievements of many seemingly unpromising youths who were trained in his school."

So he believed in the mastery of the art of public discourse. Indeed his addresses have been analyzed by teachers of the psychology of oratory as models of the perfection of that art. We quote again from Dean Turnbull, "Power of expression was always recognized by this master teacher as being vitally important for ministers of the Gospel. He encouraged the acquirement of good English and unaffected oratory. His delight in the budding eloquence of each group of graduates was unbounded. He used to say that the human voice was the rarest of instruments at God's disposal when once its powers were fully realized and yielded to the Master."

In an Editorial in *Wonderful Word* Rev. W. Leon Tucker gave this apt description of one of the outstanding qualities of his preaching: "He was a minstrel—a spiritual minstrel; preaching was melodious and musical when it fell from his lips. His voice was a wonderful vehicle for his message. It was full, resonant, and triumphant. The very sway of his body was poetic and passionate. He was like a reed shaken by the wind of the Holy Ghost. While multitudes were going broader, he was always going deeper. He was a poet preacher. His poems belong to the first rank of Christian poetry. Rhyme and rhythm were part of his refined nature."

It was the prophetic aspect of his ministry that left the deepest impression. Henry W. Frost, Director of the China Inland Mission, testifies to this. "In my young manhood I attended Dr. Simpson's services. The dew of youth was on his brow, and the unction of the Holy One was peculiarly with him. It was no wonder that great blessings followed his ministry and that I was a sharer in it. I can never be other than grateful for the lessons learned at that time in his ministry." "The man and his message," Rev. W. H. Chandler says, "won my heart to a deeper life in the Lord. For years I had been interested in the experience of holiness; but when I learned that the indwelling Christ was the secret of holiness, my heart found rest." That great English preacher, F. B. Meyer, D.D., who ministered with him both in America and England, says: "He leaves a trail of light which will linger long as an inspiration and appeal." Dr. C. I. Scofield, who was even nearer to him, wrote this tribute: "It has been my privilege to know with some measure of intimacy the greater preachers and men of God of the present time. Among these, and with no disparagement to any, I count Dr. A. B. Simpson the foremost in power to reach the depths of the human soul. And his message was so bathed in love that it was always redolent of the personality of Him whom having not seen we love." Pastor F. E. Marsh gives this testimony: "It was my happy privilege to be Associate Pastor with him of the Gospel Tabernacle. His home-going is a personal loss. The impress of his character as a man of God is unique. His ministry was unparalleled. He was not only clear in testimony, but there was a tenderness in tone and sympathy in expression which went to the heart."

Dr. Simpson was a prophet to the prophets. Even in

his early days he left deep impressions upon his fellow-ministers, as is shown by the testimony of Dr. W. H. Hincks of Toronto, given some years ago before the Guelph Methodist Conference where he stated that he was very thankful for religious impressions that came to him while sitting under the ministry of Rev. A. B. Simpson of Knox Church, Hamilton. In his later years he became pre-eminently a preacher's preacher. Referring to Dr. Simpson in one of his addresses, Dr. T. DeWitt Talmadge said that he had recently attended a meeting in a New York City Church, with a dingy auditorium and a very ordinary looking crowd of people, with nothing æsthetic or emotional in the service; but that before the minister had been preaching three minutes he felt that his head and shoulders had been lifted into heaven. One day when Dwight L. Moody was in New York, he said to his friend, Dr. A. T. Pierson, "Pierson, I have just been down to hear A. B. Simpson preach. No one gets at my heart like that man."

Paul Rader, who has had the distinguished honor of being the successor of both Moody and Simpson, thus speaks of him: "He was the greatest heart preacher I ever listened to. He preached out of his own rich dealings with God. The Word was ever new and fresh in his own experience and messages. I thank God with all my heart for what his life and messages have been to me and to multitudes of others."

Dr. Wilbert W. White of the Bible Teachers' Training School, New York City, sent this message to the memorial service: "For years I read with personal profit the messages of Dr. Simpson. Many of them are filed away for future reference. Only the other day, in the study of Habakkuk, I came across a refreshing suggestion of his concerning the outlook of faith, the patience of faith, and the joy of faith." Dr. Marquis, of the same school, said at the Sunday memorial service in the Tabernacle: "Not only was Dr. Simpson a man of God, he was a great preacher, the greatest whose voice has been heard in New York City in twenty-five years. And more, he was an artist in the way of treating the truth. His voice, manner, gestures, his marshaling of facts—they were the method of one who was an expert in the art of expounding God's Word to the people. What made his natural gifts and his spiritual gifts as an interpreter of the truth effective were, of course, his deeply spiritual life, his profound conviction of the truth, his passion for souls, and his great faith in God."

William Dayton Roberts, D.D., of Temple Presbyterian Church, Philadelphia, said after one of his visits, "We shall not hear another such message until he returns to this city."

It was said of the Great Teacher that "the common people heard him gladly." In this Dr. Simpson was like his Master. His closest friend and associate, Dr. Henry Wilson, himself a philosopher, said: "There are other great preachers who are clear without being so deep. But Dr. Simpson is both deep and clear, leading the profoundest thinkers into the deepest things of God, and at the same time so clear and simple as to be easily understood by even the uneducated."

This quality impressed others. *The Atlanta Constitution* made this comment: "His style of preaching is childlike in its simplicity, and he avoids anything like redundancy. He is fond of simple words and short sentences, and yet he makes them serve as vehicles for profound thought and sublime theology. A large number of children were scattered about in the congregation yesterday morning, and the eloquent divine seemed to have no difficulty in holding their individual attention."

Rev. Edward B. Shaw, D. D., who was one of the boys in Dr. Simpson's congregation in Hamilton, tells this story: "Waiting for a train in a little village in Massachusetts, I got into conversation with a flagman. There was no mistaking that he was Irish. 'Did you ever hear a man named Simpson?' said he. 'Yes,' I said, 'I have known him many years.' 'And how do you like him?' he asked. 'Very much,' said I, 'he is a great preacher.' 'Sure,' he said, 'I could sit on the point of a picket fence twenty-four hours and listen to that man'."

His ideal of preaching is shown in a story he told of the celebrated philosopher David Hume: "Some one took David Hume to hear one of the most popular preachers of the time, and when asked afterwards whether he liked it, replied, 'That man preached as if he did not believe a word of it.' He went to hear John Brown, a devoted Scotch preacher, on the same afternoon and came away saying, 'That man preaches as though he got the sentence straight from heaven, as if Jesus was standing at his elbow, and as though he said, 'Lord, what will I say next?' That was the testimony of an infidel to a man that preached as the oracle of God, the voice of God, the messenger of divine revelation."

Dr. Lowe Fletcher, who has known Dr. Simpson since his association with him in Louisville forty-four years ago, closes a short life sketch with a paragraph which expresses beautifully the thought which is in many a heart:

"The story of Dr. Simpson's life work cannot be told in simple words, and not until the men and women saved through his ministry come one by one from the dark Soudan, the thickets of Tibet, the shores of the Congo and Euphrates, and from the remotest places of earth, and sit down with him in the Kingdom of God, will there be an opportunity for even an approximate estimate of the far reaches of his earthly ministry."

CHAPTER 20

LEADER AND FRIEND

THERE have been many great leaders, but leader-friends have been few. The crowning glory of A. B. Simpson's leadership was that he was a friend of man. He loved the man next to him, he loved men, and he loved mankind.

After what has been written it seems to be needless to speak of his leadership. His life story is more eloquent than words. Yet there are features that may be outlined to make the picture more complete.

A. B. Simpson was an apostle. No, he was not a thirteenth apostle, nor a fiftieth. There were twelve apostles, chosen by Jesus Christ as witnesses to his life, death, and resurrection, and there will not be another. Neither do we mean that he was in an apostolic succession, commissioned by men, who, with their predecessors back to the twelve, had been themselves successively commissioned. Such men do not claim to be apostles. But there were apostles before the twelve and after them. Barnabas is called an apostle in the Lystra story. And "There was a man, sent from God, whose name was John." Our verb "sent" does not do justice to the word John the Apostle used of John the Baptist. It is the verbal form of apostle and means *sent on a commission*. An apostle is a commissioner from the court of heaven. Such a man was A. B. Simpson.

Only a man divinely commissioned could have done what Dr. Simpson accomplished. False apostles have for a time wrought mighty works, but they did it by the skillful use of human agencies, if not by preternatural power. This man did not employ the means men use to achieve leadership. He neither exalted himself nor would he allow others to exalt him. He did not exploit the public. The tricks of the advertiser he despised. He did not lay stress on organization; in fact, he determinedly opposed the introduction of much machinery. In his dedicatory address of the Madison Avenue Tabernacle he said: "I am afraid of human greatness; I am afraid of the triumphs of human praise; I am glad to have the work of God beginning in lowliness." But he believed that God had sent him on a definite mission and for a specific ministry and lived and loved and labored in the unconquerable courage and invincible strength of a true apostle.

A. B. Simpson was a pathfinder. Like Abram "he went, out, not knowing whither he went." Many so-called leaders follow the beaten path. The really great leaders blaze a new trail. Columbus crossed the uncharted sea. LaSalle and Mackenzie opened a continent. Lincoln led in the liberation of a race. Here we have a man whose life work seemed to be to push on alone where his fellows had seen nothing to explore, and where the multitude would not follow. He dared to ask his fashionable Louisville congregation to follow him from a comfortable church home to a theatre that they might together reach the masses. Single-handed he launched the first pictorial missionary magazine. Alone he stepped out in the great metropolis to find a way to the hardened hearts of multitudes. With a Gideon's band he attempted to take unevangelized continents for Christ. He revived methods untried or forgotten since the days of the apostles. He found a way through the clash of creeds to Christ Himself, restoring mysticism to Pauline purity, saving sanctification from the plane of self-perfection, placing healing on terms of abiding in and intimate fellowship with Christ, and giving a new note of strenuous service to the song of welcome to the coming King. These were "The Old Paths" but overgrown with the theological weeds of centuries.

As a leader he was unique. One of his fellow-workers has written: "Neither he nor his work can be explained upon scientific principles. The organization itself is the simplest and, I may say, the most fragile possible. It holds together by a mysterious, invisible bond. Its members are neither received into nor cast out from its fellowship. They simply are or they are not. The methods of finance are the same." Dr. C. I. Scofield adds this word, "With this seasoned and mature gift was united a power of detail and of organization that made him unique among the great Christian leaders of the day." His successor, Rev. Paul Rader, says "No man ever held an organization with as light a hand as did Dr. Simpson."

He had his own way of enlisting and training workers. He never asked a man to join his organization nor held out inducements to attract him. He knew that the path that he was marking out was too rugged for any but such as had caught his own vision. But when he met a man after his own heart, great was his delight. At the first convention in Binghamton, N. Y., he met Rev. W. T. MacArthur. At midnight Mrs. Simpson called from the window beneath which the two preachers were walking up and down. Mr. Simpson replied, "Yes, dear, I'll be up soon, but I've caught a rare bird this time." Few indeed were the conventions which he held, especially in the early days, where new workers were not enlisted. The city of Toronto alone gave him Dr. R. H. Glover, now the Foreign Secretary, Rev. Robert Jaffray, whose persistent faith planted a mission in Indo-China, and many other missionaries and home workers. When a young student in that city said to him after one of his powerful appeals, "Dr. Simpson, if you have a hard place, please send me to it," he secured another recruit by simply replying, "My dear boy, we have lots of hard places." No one ever knew better than he how to awaken the heroism in young hearts.

When they were enlisted, this leader put recruits to the test. It has been the practice of the Society to turn missionary candidates loose in some untried home field or before some half-closed door. If they stood the test and proved that they were not only soul winners but good soldiers of Jesus Christ who could endure hardness, Dr. Simpson and the Board believed that they would succeed on the foreign field. Many of these young men and women have looked into a penniless purse and an empty cupboard, and sung the nursery rhyme about "Old Mother Hubbard" to the tune of "Praise God from Whom All Blessings Flow."

A business man, who has been one of his great admirers, said recently, "Dr. Simpson had many followers but few disciples." The missionary to whom this was said replied that there were three hundred men and women on the foreign field who were his disciples indeed and that his spiritual following in mission lands were numbered by thousands. This is borne out by the testimony of Dr. George F. Pentecost, who, just before he finished his course, wrote "I have met some of his missionaries in various parts of the pagan world and they all seem animated by his spirit." We need not go to the distant shores to find his disciples. Dr. George H. Sandison, of *The Christian Herald,* who knew him and his work intimately, said "He preached the full Gospel in simple yet effective language and gathered about him as his aids men who were like-minded, and who followed his methods with success."

The test of leadership is time. Long ago, Gamaliel said, "Let these men alone." He knew that time would tell the story. A prominent minister of New York suggested at one of the October conventions that, as there was no one like Dr. Simpson to continue the leadership of the movement, a large endowment fund should be raised to insure the perpetuation of the work. Dr. Simpson said nothing and did nothing. He believed with Gamaliel that if the work were of God, nothing could overthrow it. How he rejoiced during the last months of his life, when he had no active part in leadership, at the reports of largely increased missionary offerings and marvelous progress on the foreign field. The fact that the year that has passed since he was laid to rest has been the most prosperous in the history of the work gives its own witness.

Some have concluded that because a great work had developed around the personality of Dr. Simpson, he must have been autocratic. Those who really knew him smile at the suggestion. Rev. A. E. Funk, who has been longer and more closely associated with him than any other man now living, says, "He trusted those in charge of the different institutions and left them free to exercise their own gifts"; and to this statement every man who has been intimate with him will subscribe. When some one asked a leading member of the Board if it were true that

Dr. Simpson dominated everything, he replied somewhat indignantly, "Nothing is ever passed in the Board without full discussion and an open vote. But," he added, and herein he showed his own quality of greatness, "if he sat in my place, and I were president, he would still be the controlling factor."

This suggests that his leadership was most manifest when he was surrounded, as he so often was in public, by the great men of his day. He never suffered by comparison. At one of the Old Orchard conventions, the platform was particularly strong. When it was over, some one remarked that though the messages had been in unusual power, Dr. Simpson's series of addresses was the great feature of the convention.

His associates loved Dr. Simpson. He did not preserve much of his correspondence, but a Christmas letter from Dr. Henry Wilson, written in 1907 very shortly before his death, found among Dr. Simpson's papers, shows the tender attachment between these two great men.

"My dear Mr. Simpson:

Only a brief, true-hearted word of love, sweetening and deepening the years and the coming and going of these holy seasons—love born from above for yourself personally, to whom I owe more than I can ever express; love for Mrs. Simpson in these days of heavy burden-bearing, and for all the family; and praise for the privilege of having with you a part in the work dearer to us than life. More than ever

Yours in Christ,

HENRY WILSON."

Few men were more intimately associated with Dr. Simpson than Dr. F. W. Farr, who says: "An apostolic man has passed from earth to heaven. His mighty faith, his flaming zeal, his tireless devotion, his abounding labors, place him among the great leaders of the Christian Church. His enduring monument is seen in the multitudes of transformed and consecrated lives the world around and in the splendid heroism of devoted missionaries in every land. Measured by the standards of eternity, his was a great and noble life."

Paul Rader was only voicing his own experience when he said of Dr. Simpson's disciples, "They did not follow *him*. He was abandoned to God, and they saw that he walked with his Lord. They, too, in this abandonment, found the joy of this faith life in the all faithful One."

Dr. S. D. Gordon, author of "Quiet Talks," speaks of him in his own distinctive manner: "Gentle, cultured, scholarly, Spirit-filled, he left the smoother rhythm of the regular pastorate for the very difficult special ministry in answer to the Master's call, and that ministry was blessed immeasurably to tens of thousands of communions of the United States and Canada and reached out in the far corners of the earth. The memory of it and of him will be fragrant down here until he returns with his Lord in the air for the blessed new order of things which will likely be very soon."

Mr. Wm. E. Blackstone, in expressing his deep regret that failing strength and great pressure in his own work of world-evangelization, prevented him from writing a chapter of this biography, said "I cannot express to you what a joy it would be to me if I could write a suitable chapter for this book. I loved Dr. Simpson, I loved his life and ministry, and the work which he has so greatly promoted both in spiritual life and in advanced foreign mission work "

At the memorial service Mr. Charles G. Trumbull, Editor of *The Sunday School Times,* revealed one of the secrets of the regard felt for Dr. Simpson. "I had a very real need in my own life, and talked with Dr. Simpson at Old Orchard about it. He listened with all love, and sympathy, and understanding, and explained to me the meaning of the committal of things to God. Then we knelt and he prayed. And I can never forget, even in eternity, his prayer for me that day as he talked with God, talked to God *for me*. A man at that time with heavy responsibilities for multitudes of persons in every part of this earth, with the names of many, many missionaries in his mind and on his heart for his prayer stewardship, loved ones in the home circle, loved ones here in the Gospel Tabernacle, and, with uncounted obligations in every direction, was just for that moment talking to God as though he had no other responsibility except this one person who had come to him for help. And as he prayed, his whole being was simply vibrating with the spiritual consciousness of his fellowship with God at that moment for the need of a brother. He was laying hold of God because I had laid hold of him for that very need. And, oh, can you understand the blessing that God poured out at that time into my life just because dear Dr. Simpson gave himself wholly, unreservedly to that intercession for one person at the throne of God?"

There were other secrets. Evangelist Charles Inglis, who has preached on three continents, says, "He was the most gracious man I ever knew." A state superintendent of the Alliance, Rev. I. Patterson, writes, "One of the greatest secrets of his successful life and ministry was his humility." Mrs. A. A. Kirk, for many years Superintendent of Women in the Missionary Institute,

15

found that "He was always most courteous and humble in times of ministry, quickly acknowledging the gifts of others." A home worker, Rev. H. E. Cottrell, recalled with what diffidence he "went to the hotel to meet Dr. Simpson, but he put me at ease at once. He reminded me of the Psalmist's words, 'Thy gentleness hath made me great'."

Rev. E. M. Burgess, a cultured and gifted leader of Alliance work among the colored people, sent this special message: "During the October Convention of 1915, while there at his invitation to sing, I heard him publicly express his deep love for our people, especially in the homeland, and of the South in particular, and urged the people to pray that the time would speedily come when the Lord would thrust forth Rev. E. M. Collett, Dr. C. S. Morris, and myself as an evangelistic party to tour the country, spreading the full gospel message among our people. This utterance received a very hearty and fervent assent. On behalf of our people, and at the request of some of the leaders of our branches, please record the fact of Dr. Simpson's great and sincere love for our people and the inestimable loss his home-going has meant to us."

If the great men who knew him loved Dr. Simpson, the average man and the poor and unlettered held him in equal esteem. Not only in his own congregation, but wherever he went in conventions, the very attitude of the people manifested their love and devotion. In the next chapter Dr. Turnbull will tell of the regard with which he was held by his students. His missionaries held him in tenderest affection. His God-speed and his warm hand-clasp and word of welcome cheered the recruit and heartened the returning veteran. When on some far-away field a weary missionary received a personal letter written in his own careful handwriting, tears would fall that so great and busy a man at so great a distance had time and thought for the lonely messenger of the cross. The children loved him. Dr. Shaw has told us of the effect upon him when, as a boy, the hand of the young Hamilton pastor was laid upon his head. But what would many of the younger generation tell of the effect of Dr. Simpson's patriarchal hand, his fatherly smile, and his companionable word. Truly, he was a friend of man. One might almost think that he had been in the mind of our American poet when he wrote:

> "Let me live in a house by the side of the road,
>   And be a friend to man."

Here is Dr. Simpson's own explanation of his influence. "If I have ever done anyone any good, it was not I, but Christ in me."

CHAPTER *21*

IN MEMORIAM

"So when a great man dies,
    For years beyond our ken,
The light he leaves behind him lies
    Upon the paths of men."

WHEN General Allenby captured Jerusalem in December, 1917, Dr. Simpson was in Chicago on a convention tour. He went immediately to his room, overcome with emotion, and on his knees praised God for an hour. He had been watching the Jewish clock for forty years, and now its warning chime announced that the great hour of the redeemed was at hand. He gave a powerful address on "The Capture of Jerusalem" in Moody Tabernacle, which he repeated in his own pulpit on his return to New York.

In the following January he was announced as one of the chief speakers at a Jewish mission conference in Chicago, but after the conference had commenced he wired his life-long friend, Mrs. T. C. Rounds, Superintendent of the Chicago Hebrew Mission, who was secretary of the convention, expressing his regrets that he found himself unable to attend. It was a great disappointment, for every one knew that a message for the hour was burning in his heart.

During the rest of the winter he engaged in very little public ministry, and most of his other duties were laid aside. He submitted to urgent solicitation and, accompanied by Mrs. Simpson, spent a few weeks with his friends of other days at Clifton Springs, New York. He did not, as some have suggested, take medical treatment. Dr. Sanders of the sanitarium was an old friend and a former attendant at the Tabernacle, and thoroughly understood Dr. Simpson's position.

When the Annual Council of The Christian and Missionary Alliance assembled at Nyack in May, 1918, Dr. Simpson called upon Mr. Ulysses Lewis, Vice-President of the Society, to preside, though he himself attended most of the sessions. During this Council, as stated in an earlier chapter, he committed his business affairs to his brethren for settlement. This was not only a great personal relief to him but also proved that he never had any desire to build up an estate for his personal or family interest, and enabled one of the speakers at the memorial service to make the public announcement that Dr. Simpson left no legacy but the will and work of God—the richest heritage ever bequeathed to family or friends.

Dr. Simpson had lived, as he tells us in the story of his life crisis, a lonely life. One of the secrets of his success was that he had taken his difficulties directly to the Lord, and even his immediate family knew little of the burdens which he bore from day to day. He attempted to continue to meet the pressure that was upon him during the early months of his physical decline as he had always done. The great adversary, against whose kingdom he had so valiantly warred, attacked him in his weakness and succeeded in casting a cloud over his spirit.

Even yet he did not call his brethren to his spiritual help until one of them, a short time after the Council, asked for the privilege of staying with him at night, at which time the pressure was most severe. For several weeks one or other of the brethren enjoyed what they will ever regard as the unspeakable privilege of this intimate fellowship. He would kneel at his bedside with the one who was with him and pour out his heart unto the Lord. After retiring they would lie in sweet communion, quoting the great promises of Scripture and softly singing the hymns which have been endeared to the Church, or the yet richer Psalms of David in the old Scottish metrical version, which he, and at least some of these friends, had sung in childhood. When the brother would say, "Dr. Simpson, you must sleep now," he would say, "Yes, yes, but we must have another word of prayer." By this time that rich consciousness of the indwelling Christ, in which for forty years he had never failed to compose himself for sleep, had returned in some measure to him, and presently he would be sleeping as a child. When he awakened in the morning, addressing the one beside him with the affectionate familiarity of a spiritual father, he would express the hope that he had not disturbed him. Again in "psalms and hymns and spiritual songs" the day would be begun, till the brother left for his daily duty. So several weeks were passed.

One day two of the brethren, who had been greatly stirred by the Holy Spirit for his complete deliverance, bowed with him in his library. They prayed a prayer into which he earnestly sought to enter with a real Amen. The brethren knew, as did Dr. Simpson, that they wrestled "not against flesh and blood, but against principalities, against powers, against the rulers of the darkness of this world, against spiritual wickedness in high places." Presently they knew that victory had been given, but they longed and hoped that it also might mean perfect physical deliverance. Before they rose from their knees he said, "Boys, I do not seem to be able to take quite all

that you have asked. You seem to have outstripped me—
but Jesus is so real"; and he began to talk to his Lord
as only a man who has known the intimate love-life of the
Man in the glory can do.

From that hour no one ever heard Dr. Simpson speak
of the enemy, and to the last those who met him in the
Tabernacle or at the headquarters in New York, or at
Old Orchard, where he went soon afterward, or later in
his own home and bedchamber, were conscious of even
a richer aroma of Christ than that sweet fragrance which
for so many years had surrounded him.

His marvelous ministry of prayer was revivified. His
friend, Rev. W. T. MacArthur, who a short time before
had spent two or three days with him, returned un-
heralded. Dr. Simpson met him at the door and said,
"Well, Mac, you have come to pray for me again." "No,
Brother Simpson, I have come to ask you to pray for
me." "That is a very gracious way of putting it," he
replied. "Not at all; it is the truth. I have carried my
old sermon barrel till I am sick of it. I must have a fresh
anointing." "Oh, then, if that is so," said Dr. Simpson,
"we will go right into my study." That night a series of
messages were born in the preacher's soul, and those who
heard him that summer knew that fresh oil had been
poured upon him.

Nor was Mr. MacArthur the only one who found his
way to this man of God for just such an anointing. One
after another of the brethren met him quietly and alone
with the same result. He seemed to be pouring out upon
these disciples something of the gift which had so enriched his own ministry.

Perhaps the most memorable of these occasions was
that which occurred when Paul Rader came from Chi-

cago to New York for a night of prayer and special con-
sultation with the Board concerning his relation to the
work. We will let Mr. Rader tell the story.

"Never will I forget a night a few months ago. Dr.
Simpson was occupying a room at Headquarters across
the hall from the Board meeting which he was unable
to attend. At the close of the meeting I went into his
room with Brother Senft and Brother Lewis. He put
out his arm, and we knelt to pray. Oh, such a prayer!
He started in thanksgiving for the early days, and swept
the past in waves of praise at each step; then to the present; then on to the future—the prophetic vision was
marvelous. We were all with upturned, tear-stained faces
praising God together with him as by faith we followed
him to the mountain and viewed the Promised Land. He
was so sure the Alliance was born in the heart of God.
He lay there in a burst of praise, sure that God could
carry it forward. He knew his physical life was closing.
So, reverently he lifted his hands as if passing the work
over to God who had carried it all these days."

Perhaps Mr. Rader was the only one of the brethren
who dared to claim a double portion of his spirit. Those
of us who saw him that day when he came out from that
prayer scene realized that in his inner consciousness,
whether he confessed it to himself or not, Paul Rader
knew that the mantle was falling upon him. All the way
to Nyack he would answer us only in monosyllables; and
when he stood before the students that night, the natural
man which had dazzled many an audience had disappeared,
and for that night he stood in brokenness, quietly uttering
a message which went to the depths of many a heart,
though he himself felt that he had failed.

During the winter of 1918-1919 Dr. Simpson spent a

considerable part of the time at Headquarters in New York, and attended most of the meetings in the Tabernacle. He started a daily prayer meeting and once ventured to address the Friday meeting. He attended the great Prophetic Conference in Carnegie Hall, delighting in the fellowship of such old friends as Dr. W. B. Riley, Dr. James M. Gray, Dr. George William Carter, Mr. Charles G. Trumbull, and many others. The chairman of one of the meetings called upon him to lead in prayer, and though the audience could see that his strength had failed greatly, when he began to pour out his heart to God a hush fell over the vast assembly, and men realized anew that in real prayer

> "Heaven comes down our souls to greet
> While glory crowns the mercy seat."

Dr. and Mrs. Simpson spent the early springtime on the beautiful Nyack hillside in Dean Turnbull's residence near the Institute, to the great delight of the students, and later returned to their own home a little farther down the hill.

Just before the Annual Council in May he suffered a slight stroke of paralysis, which prevented him and Mrs. Simpson from going to Toccoa where the Council was held that year; but he recovered so rapidly that none of the brethren was detained at Nyack. He sent this telegram to the Council: "Beloved brethren assembled in Council at Toccoa: I regret not being able to meet you this year to look over the blessing of the year gone by. Although turmoil and strife have ruled the world, God has held us by His mighty hand from the many trials and evils which have surrounded us. Blessing has been poured out upon the work and the workers as they have been guided by Him. We praise His name forever. My prayer is that God shall rule this blessed work which was begun in sacrifice and consecration to Him, for the spreading of the Gospel into all lands. I hope soon to meet you all again as He will. My text today is John 11:4—'This sickness is not unto death, but for the glory of God.' We are with you in spirit if not in body."

When the delegates returned, they found Dr. Simpson recovered almost to his condition previous to the stroke. He passed through the summer with little change, being about his own home and graciously receiving the few special friends who were privileged to call upon him. His son, Howard, who had been in the Canadian army in France, returned and spent some months at home, but in the late summer accepted a business position in Montreal. His daughter, Margaret, came frequently from New York and his older daughter, Mabel, also came from Hamilton in the early autumn to visit him.

During these months Mrs. Simpson watched over her beloved husband with the utmost devotion, and was wonderfully sustained from day to day by God's unfailing grace. Dr. Simpson received all these loving ministries with his usual graciousness but made no needless demands on those who cared for him.

On Tuesday, October 28, he spent the morning on his veranda and received a visit from Judge Clark, of Jamaica, conversing freely, and praying fervently for Rev. and Mrs. George H. A. McClare, our Alliance missionaries in Jamaica, and for the missionaries in other fields, who were always in his mind. After the Judge left him he suddenly lost consciousness and was carried to his room. His daughter Margaret and a little group of friends watched by the bedside with Mrs. Simpson till his great spirit took leave of his worn out body and returned to God who gave it, early on Wednesday morning, October 29, 1919.

Mr. Howard Simpson and Mrs. Brennan and her two daughters, Marjorie and Katherine, hastened from Canada, Mrs. Gordon Simpson, a widowed daughter-in-law, and her daughters, Misses Joyce, Ruth, Wilhelmina and Anna, and her son Albert came from New York City, and a nephew, Dr. James Simpson, of Ridgefield Park, N. J., was also present.

Mrs. Simpson received hundreds of letters and telegrams from all parts of the world and many messages of sympathy were sent officially to *The Christian and Missionary Alliance* and *The Alliance Weekly* from kindred organizations.

The Congo Mission wrote through its executive committee: "The news of Dr. Simpson's home-going came to us as a shock. We had been praying and hoping that the Lord would restore him to health and grant him yet many years of service in directing the world-wide Alliance work which was so dear to his heart and to which he gave himself so unselfishly and untiringly. May our heavenly Father, the God of all comfort, sustain you in your separation and sorrow. As a mission and as part of the Alliance family we bear you up in our prayers and trust that the Lord will continue to use you in this work, which we know is also dear to your heart."

Rev. E. A. Kilbourne, of the Oriental Missionary Society, Japan, sent this message: "His influence was not confined to the ranks of The Christian and Missionary Alliance, but preachers, missionaries, editors, and people of all denominations have been moved and stirred by his untiring zeal for the cause of Christ in all the world.

How glad I am that I was permitted to sit at his feet. His inspiring messages have always stirred my soul."

Several leaders in Jewish missions sent tender messages, among whom were Rev. Samuel Wilkinson, of the Mildmay Mission to the Jews, London; Rev. S. B. Rohold, superintendent of the Mission to the Jews, Toronto; Rev. Thomas M. Chalmers, of the Jewish Mission, New York; and Rev. Maurice Ruben, of the New Covenant Mission, Pittsburgh, who said: "It is with the deepest feeling of a personal loss that I wish to express my innermost sympathy to all the Alliance family in the departure of their beloved leader. Truly a prince in Israel has fallen. Dr. Simpson was one among thousands, and he will leave a vacancy that will not easily be filled."

Rev. Henry W. Frost, director of the China Inland Mission, wrote that "Dr. Simpson belonged to the whole Church of Christ. His ministries overflowed boundaries and went out into every place. It is a true mark of a Spirit-filled man. I speak also for the members of the China Inland Mission in expressing to The Christian and Missionary Alliance our heartfelt sympathy in their great loss."

The president of the Toronto *Globe,* Mr. W. G. Jaffray, sent this personal word: "The Christian and Missionary Alliance stands as a monument of his devotion to God's purpose for him in this life. Eternity alone will show the full results of his earthly ministry. Both myself and my family have experienced his loving sympathy and help in times gone by."

Other brief extracts show the regard in which he was held by the great men of the Church. Prof. W. H. Griffith Thomas, D.D., said: "In the death of Dr. Simpson it is literally true to say that a great man has fallen in

Israel. For many years I have followed his work with keen interest and genuine admiration." His old friend, Dr. James M. Gray, D.D., Dean of the Moody Bible Institute, wrote: "I knew Dr. Simpson before The Christian Alliance was formed, and my feelings toward him have passed from wonder and admiration to the deepest confidence and love." Dr. George H. Sandison of *The Christian Herald,* who knew him intimately at Nyack, and as a fellow editor, said that "His epitaph is written in the hearts of countless multitudes at home and abroad. I can think of no one in this age who has done more effectual, self-denying service for Christ and His Gospel than Albert B. Simpson. It will be one of the dearest memories of my life that I had the honor and pleasure of calling him my friend." Dr. D. McTavish, in whose church in Toronto many of the Alliance conventions were held, adds this word: "Rev. A. B. Simpson was a man definitely laid hold of by God to do a marvelous work. He was a great gospel preacher, a great defender of 'the faith once for all delivered unto the saints'; a great missionary advocate and a great-hearted Christian friend. We shall sorely miss his genial presence, but what a glorious welcome awaited such a splendidly invested life." Dr. W. B. Riley, of The First Baptist Church, Minneapolis, sent this word of mingled sorrow and hope: "It was a great personal grief to me to know of the going of Dr. A. B. Simpson. For more than twenty-five years I have known him and my admiration increased with the acquaintance. Truly, the cause of Christ is the poorer for his departure, but how much richer for his sacrifices and services of love. We join with a host of friends in expressing congratulations to his dear wife and family on the great life he lived, and our condolence on the separation which, let us trust, will be cut short by the soon-coming of his Lord."

Four simple and impressive services were held in connection with the memorial. The first of these was in the Gospel Tabernacle, New York, on Sunday morning, November 2, at which several of the church officers and members of the Board of The Christian and Missionary Alliance gave loving tributes to their beloved friend. Dr. Marquis of the Bible Teachers' Training School, who was present, was called to the platform and gave a brief but most appreciative impromptu address which is quoted elsewhere. On Sunday afternoon three hundred Institute students lined the winding pathway leading up the hillside from the Simpson home to the Missionary Institute, while other students carried the casket to the Institute chapel. An informal service was held in the evening at which many testimonies were given as to the influence of the life of Dr. Simpson, the founder of the institution, upon the students and the faculty.

On Monday afternoon a more formal tribute was given by Rev. R. A. Forrest, Rev. A. E. Funk, Rev. Henri DeVries, Rev. T. P. Gates, and Dr. J. Gregory Mantle. Dr. Mantle told how the vergers of St. Paul's Cathedral show to travelers the sculptured monuments of Britain's greatest sons. Finally the verger points out a little tablet on which is inscribed:

> "Sir Christopher Wren,
> Born in 1631,
> Died in 1723;
> If you seek his monument, look around."

"So," said Dr. Mantle, "would I say of this man—'If you seek his monument, look around'."

The principal service was held in the Gospel Tabernacle, New York, on Tuesday at noon. So many desired to attend that admittance was by ticket. The members of the Board of The Christian and Missionary Alliance, the elders of the Gospel Tabernacle, the faculty of the Missionary Institute, many missionaries and home workers of the Alliance, and representative ministers of the Gospel from various denominations filled the platform. They included many of the disciples who were now to carry forward the work he had begun. Mr. Ulysses Lewis, of Atlanta, Georgia, presided. Rev. F. H. Senft offered the invocation; Rev. J. E. Jaderquist read the Scripture; and Rev. E. D. Whiteside led in a tender intercessory prayer. Mrs. Margaret Buckman, daughter of Dr. Simpson, sang one of his unpublished hymns, *The Upward Calling*.

"A Voice is calling me, a hand has grasped me,
By cords unseen my soul is upward drawn;
My heart has answered to that upward calling,
I clasp the hand that lifts and leads me on.

"I'm turning from the past that lies behind me,
I'm reaching forth unto the things before;
I've caught the taste of life's eternal fountains,
And all my being longs and thirsts for more.

"A brooding Presence hovers o'er my spirit,
The Heavenly Dove my heart doth softly woo;
I catch bright visions of my heavenly calling
And all there is for me to be and do.

"A mystic glory lingers all around me,
And all the air breathes out the eternal spring;
I feel the pulses of the new creation,
And all things whisper of the coming King.

"And in my heart I hear the Spirit's whisper,
 'The Bridegroom cometh, hasten to prepare!'
And with my vessels filled and lamps all burning
I'm going out to meet Him in the air."

Messages were read from Dr. Robert E. Speer, Secretary of the Presbyterian Board of Foreign Missions, and Dr. Wilbert W. White, of the Bible Teachers' Training School, who were both out of the city. Rev. Edward H. Emett was present and spoke as Dr. White's personal representative. Rev. Kenneth Mackenzie, the first minister in New York City to stand with Mr. Simpson on his platform when he began this ministry; Dr. Edward B. Shaw, of Monroe, New York, a Sunday-school boy in Mr. Simpson's first pastorate, and Mr. Charles G. Trumbull, Editor of *The Sunday School Times*, represented the larger circle of the Christian Church and spoke feelingly of what Dr. Simpson's life and testimony had meant to themselves and to the Church at large. Rev. P. W. Philpott, of Hamilton, Ont.; Rev. J. D. Williams, of St. Paul, Minn.; Rev. W. M. Turnbull, of Nyack, and Rev. A. E. Thompson, of Jerusalem, all members of the Board, gave testimonies on behalf of the Alliance constituency at home and abroad. The last message was a most touching tribute from Rev. Paul Rader, Vice President of The Christian and Missionary Alliance. Perhaps no minister in the great metropolis had ever been so truly honored in his memorial service as was this man who, thirty-eight years before, had dared to step out alone on the promises of God and, like Caleb of old, "wholly follow the Lord."

The funeral cortege proceeded from the Gospel Tabernacle to Woodlawn Cemetery where Dr. Simpson's body was placed in a vault. The family had intended that his last earthly resting place should be in the family plot in Hamilton, Ont., but graciously consented to the urgent request that his body should be interred on the beautiful hillside at Nyack, near the Missionary Institute. Some one had suggested that each of the sixteen mission fields send a stone, engraved in the native language, to be built into a simple but unique monument.

On Friday, May 21, 1920, at the closing of the Annual Council of The Christian and Missionary Alliance, Dr. Simpson's body was brought back to the hillside. Hundreds of delegates to the Council and other friends gathered around as the hands of men who had loved him lowered his body into the earth whence it came, and eyes looked upward knowing that the spirit had departed to be with Christ and is waiting for the day for which he had looked and longed when "the trumpet shall sound, and the dead shall be raised incorruptible, and we shall be changed," when "death is swallowed up in victory." How often he had voiced in song the hope that he would be caught up in the clouds together with the resurrected ones to meet the Lord in the air and so be forever with the Lord. He can have no regrets now for he is "with Christ which is far better" than to be here, even with friends and fellow-workers. Mrs. Simpson and many friends sorrow not as those who have no hope, for "we which are alive and remain unto the coming of the Lord shall not prevent [go before] them which are asleep" but "the dead in Christ shall rise first." As they lived here together with Christ, so then together they shall share in the power of his resurrection.

Few men since the days of Paul could so confidently say "I have fought a good fight, I have finished my course, I have kept the faith: Henceforth there is laid up for me a crown of righteousness, which the Lord, the righteous judge, shall give me at that day: and not to me only, but unto all them also that *love* his appearing."